SEX ON
Saturday Night

THE ART OF INTIMACY

BY PATRICIA HAYES SMITH

outskirts
press

DEDICATION

To Marshall Smith, my husband and loving partner for over thirty years. You were the sounding board as I wrote this book about relationships. You are and will always be my "Shining Knight" who took me to places I have never been and shared deep feelings of love that I had never felt.

Here it is, at last.

Patricia

TABLE OF CONTENTS

Prologue

THE VISION

One night, moments before sleep consumed my conscious awareness, I had a vision. I was watching a man who was lying on the ground in a desert. He appeared dead. A vulture was circling about six feet above him. I watched the vulture slowly inch closer to the man. Its beady eyes watching and waiting for the moment it could devour its prey. The vulture just kept circling. I wondered why the vulture was waiting. Suddenly, I realized the man could not be dead. If he were dead, the vulture would be feeding on its flesh.

In my vision, I walked over to the man. The vulture paid no attention to me as it continued to circle. "Wake up," I said. "Wake up! Wake up! You are not dead. Open your eyes and let this vulture see that you are still alive. Open your eyes and send this vulture away. If you do not, you will surely die, and the vulture will eat you." I desperately wanted the man to hear me, but his eyes remained closed. He could not hear me. I touched the man's hand. It was lifeless, yet I knew the man was still alive. I could feel it with every fiber of my being.

An intuitive feeling came over me. "Do not talk to the man's head. He will not hear you. He has given up hope. He has lost all faith. He has lost contact with his Spirit." When I asked that inner voice to whom I should talk, I clearly understood, "Talk to his Heart. Talk to his Spirit buried deep beneath the surface."

Moving closer to the man, I knelt beside him and said, "Hi in there. I know you are in there somewhere and can hear me. I know how you feel. My heart hurts and my thoughts have no hope when I am close to you. I know how you feel." He could not cry, but I could feel his tears and hear his thoughts. He was alive. I was right! He was feeling and thinking – and that meant he was very much alive!

I moved even closer and began talking to the man's Heart just as if his Heart were the only part that was listening. "You have a good heart," I whispered, "You have a strong heart. I can feel it. It can do anything. Your heart has not given up, only your thoughts have given up. It is your thoughts that have lost hope. Your thoughts do not know the power of your heart. Feel your heart. It is alive. It never dies. It cannot die. It is the love in you, the love you have felt, the love you feel now, and the love you will eternally feel for your loved ones. Feel it. Feel your love for your loved ones. Your love is your life, your Spirit. Bring it back. Call it back. Think of someone you love. See your loved one's face. Feel your loved one close to you. Feel your love."

Suddenly, I sensed an electrical current within the man's energy field. Encouraged by this new energy, I said, "Open your eyes. Open your eyes and scare the vulture away. Claim your life. Let your heart open your eyes and scare the ugly vulture away. Let your heart sing, 'I want to live. I am alive.' The vulture will have to go away. He will have to go away because you are alive, you want to live."

The man's eyes slowly opened as if from a deep sleep. He looked into my eyes, and I could see his heart in his eyes. I could see his Spirit. He was home in this body. He would live. I knew it. He would scare away the vulture.

Just then, I became aware of a dark cloud above the man's head. I watched as the cloud began to break up and move away until only the light of day remained. I knew these were his thoughts of hopelessness, despair, and pain leaving. His heart had won against all odds. I marveled at his magnificent heart!

He slowly got up, brushed himself off, and we both watched the vulture fly away in search of its next victim.

INTRODUCTION

***

*"When you get into a tight place and everything goes against you…
'til it seems as though you could not hold on a minute longer, never
give up then, for that is just the place and time when the tide will
turn."*

~ Harriet Beecher Stowe

COUPLES HAVE SOUGHT help with their relationships for years. Information
about sex and sexuality has been readily available as numerous professionals have shared their views. Renowned psychologist Carl Jung, celebrity
sex therapist Dr. Ruth Westheimer, and biologist and sexologist Alfred
Kinsey are among these professionals. Behavioral scientist, John Gray,
Ph.D., captured the attention of millions with his best-selling book, *Men
are from Mars, Women are from Venus.* So, since there are many published
relationship guides, what makes this book different?

Sex on Saturday Night: The Art of Intimacy provides a deeper understanding of how our emotional and spiritual health impacts our life
and our relationships. It focuses on the Sexual Self, a critical part of
our psyche that drives not only our sexuality but also our creativity and
vigor. In addition, it offers explanations for our behavior and how to

recognize and understand our partner's behavior. These are key factors in revitalizing the intimacy in one's relationship.

Our entire universe is based upon the principle of sex, the harmonious union of two opposites, a positive and negative principle, proton, and electron, male and female joined to create new life. We are sexual beings from the tip of our toes to the crown of our head. Yet, our Sexual Self is undoubtedly the most misunderstood aspect of who we are.

Regardless of gender, every human has both male and female aspects. The Sexual Self is no different. Our male aspect takes action and seeks solutions. It drives us forward. Our female aspect nurtures, births creativity, and uses intuition. This book explores our Sexual Self, its male and female aspects, and how to use the elemental powers of our sexual energy to conquer our fears, create our visions, and continually recreate ourselves in a greater image.

By delving into the inner workings of my clients, I came to realize that when hope is gone, our Heart and Spirit feel extremely distant, contributing little or nothing to our daily existence. Often trauma, setbacks or simply a deep dissatisfaction with one's life, leads us to just "go through the motions," which perpetuates the feeling of despair and helplessness. Numbness sets in, silencing our feelings. Our Heart and Spirit recede as we repress the emotional pain. As the spiral continues, we no longer find the joy and beauty in life. Then, the vulture begins to circle.

We live by the thoughts in our head rather than the feelings in our heart. We do our duty, but the passion and sense of awe for life is slipping away. We do not feel the vitality in our body or heart as we once did. While we may experience what we think is love, it is "mental love," what we think we are supposed to feel. Sadly, mental love is not fulfilling. We may say all the right things, but often, our words do not reflect our actions and certainly do not reflect our feelings.

*Sometimes it happens so gradually that we
are not even aware of our numbness.*

Problems can become overwhelming, like trying to organize a garage that is so cluttered we become immobile, not knowing where to start. It becomes impossible to function effectively in our daily activities, leaving us feeling out of control and helpless. We lose hope that anything can be done. We lose faith in ourselves and in our ability to "unclutter" our lives. When our hope and faith are gone, our loving Spirit becomes so repressed it seems as if it has left our body to seek life elsewhere. The vulture ultimately wins and devours us.

When we are in this emotional place, all aspects of our lives are impacted. Our relationships become dysfunctional; and we create coping mechanisms to survive. It is no surprise that being in this abyss negatively impacts one's sex on Saturday night.

Thus, the reason for this book.

Interestingly, the energy that drives our sexual desires also drives our creativity, our curiosity, and our desire to live a productive and fulfilling life. So, *Sex on Saturday Night: The Act of Intimacy* addresses the reasons behind our dysfunction, along with ways to release that dysfunction so that sex on Saturday night is more likely and more rewarding.

The parable in the Prologue reveals the crux of this book. The vulture symbolizes the threat to our well-being that may surface in our lives whether it be emotional trauma, dysfunction, or disease. Like a vulture, those threats circle us as though they sense that we are losing hope. Love guides the man back to his Heart and Spirit, thereby revealing the means to heal.

Our Heart is the keeper of our love. It is the foundation of intimacy. Through love, all things are possible. So, freedom from our negative thoughts, along with our understanding of those thoughts, discovered through our loving Heart and Spirit, are the factors that create and maintain a loving and intimate relationship. It is time to wake up and fully resurrect our Heart. Awareness cannot be attained through the mind. One can only experience love and joy in life and a feeling of Greater Love through the Heart.

You are the navigator of your life. You are the only one who can determine why you are here and what you will do with your life. If you never delve into the depth of your Heart, you will miss the opportunity of a lifetime.

The awakening of your Heart is the awakening of your eternal nature of Love. Love is not religious zealousness or the desires of your emotional nature. Love is constant, objective and consistently caring. It is not subject to moods. Love can evaluate clearly without opinion or judgment. It carries within it a great healing light that can transform anything that is unlike itself. It is not a thought of love or parroting what love should be. It is the pure essence of love. You must be fully in your Heart to awaken the pure essence of love. Each stage of awareness takes you into a greater depth of love and spiritual understanding. Purpose, direction, and good choices become a way of life. Only you can find the answer to the question — *what must I change in my life to feel greater peace of mind, recognize my self-value, and restore intimacy in my relationship?*

Sex on Saturday Night: The Act of Intimacy is the first step in finding your answer. The energy of that intimacy impregnates your life with the spirit of love and wisdom. It transforms a dull and disconnected existence into a life of wonder, joy, health, and gratitude, giving you a fulfilling connection to your loved ones and taking you to Higher thought.

Enjoy!

Patricia Hayes Smith

Chapter One:

THE THRILL IS GONE?

"Believe nothing because a wise man said it,
Believe nothing because it is generally held,
Believe nothing because it is written,
Believe nothing because it is said to be divine,
Believe nothing because someone else believes it
But believe only what you yourself judge to be true."

~ Buddha, 6th century B.C.

IS THE THRILL gone? Has sex on Saturday night become a thing of the past? Most relationships start out with that intense "vroom-vroom." Sexual desire is "revved" up like one would rev up a motorcycle. Sadly, many relationships lose that energy and settle into what some would call the humdrum of life. Couples are often left scratching their heads, wondering what went wrong, blaming themselves or their partners for what they perceive is "falling out of love."

Love is love. Regardless of your partnership — straight, same-sex, married, living together or any other form of commitment you may be in – we are all subject to these issues. According to the National Center for Health Statistics, marriage rates (per 1,000 population) fell from a high of 10.9 in 1972 to a low of 6.5 in 2017. It has become far more acceptable to just be in a healthy, loving, committed relationship without taking marriage vows. Commitment alone, regardless of its expression, is not a guarantee of a happy and healthy relationship.

Interestingly, we humans are hard-wired for relationships no matter what the legal or social expectations, no matter the gender pairing. It is fundamental to the propagation of the species. We thrive on "love" – or at least what we perceive to be love. We tend to enter a relationship because of love only to find that the endorphins wane and we feel empty. So, what causes us to lose the thrill?

There are a variety of reasons why relationships lose vitality. Each partner contributes, yet it is a rare couple whose emotional and spiritual health can bring harmony, and, in turn, vitality to the relationship – not impossible but rare. We do an emotional dance with our partner – he did this, so I did that, she said this, so I said that – cha, cha, cha. Our perceptions and our reactions most often stem from our own deep thoughts or childhood wounds. *To best understand your relationship and restore its vitality, it is best to first understand yourself including all your distinct parts, thoughts, feelings, and behavior.*

We will start with the basics.

THE SEXUAL SELF

We are comprised of Selves, that is, aspects or energies that each represent a component of who we are. These are the fundamental components from which our basic thoughts, feelings, intent, desires, and behavior derive. While we have a number of Selves, the Sexual Self plays a key role in the vitality in relationships – no surprise there.

While sex is an important part of our lives, our Sexual Self is about much more than just the physical act of sex. We live in a society that has narrowed the view of our Sexual Self to a penis or vagina. Our emphasis has been on its gender and the physical act of sex rather than on exploring its vast potential and role as a creator in our life. Our obsession with the physical act of sex has made one's prowess in the bedroom a measure of self-esteem. Men count their "conquests." Women must look sexy. Sex as a measure of worth stems from our fears of inadequacy. It may surprise you to know that the act of physical sex is a minute fraction of the powerful and creative abilities of our Sexual Self.

The limited understanding of our sexuality and how to express it effectively has devastated many of us with an accumulation of mixed feelings including inadequacy, helplessness, unworthiness, and fear, constantly stirring thoughts of inferiority about sexuality and the role it plays in understanding and defining the fullness of who we are. Dealing with issues of control, power, and insecurities about our sexuality causes confusion about our sexuality and our ability to express effectively in other areas of our life.

It has caused even greater problems with our interaction with life partners. Often in relationships, our "confused self" becomes involved with the "confused self" of another. In those situations, we lose sight of our boundaries, we muddle the truths about self. Our young hearts set grand expectations about relationships, resulting in disappointing experiences. Without a higher awareness, there is no recourse for our broken dreams except to blame ourselves or others. Blame does nothing to solve the confusion and feelings of helplessness that occur, especially when there are issues of betrayal or misuse of power in a loving relationship with another.

Often, our negative inward feelings harden our facade of protection and numbs our sensitivity to the very spirit of our Sexual Self, the primal force of our greatest creative power. Even worse, we cannot figure out what to do about it.

It is time to develop a new and intimate relationship with our Sexual Self, a relationship that fuels our creative endeavors and lights up our life with meaning and joy – and, in so doing, revive our loving relationships. Thinking about and using the power of our Sexual Self in such a new enlightening and fascinating way enables us to fuel our greatest creative endeavors, forever enriching our life and restoring confidence and faith in Self. So, the term "sex on Saturday night" not only describes revitalizing one's relationship with one's partner, but it also describes the birth of an emerging creativity empowered by the Sexual Self and fueled by an unending source of inspired, creative endeavors that enrich our lives and the lives of others. A healthy Sexual Self is the basis of a spiritually inspired lifestyle with a promise of love fulfilled and structured to perpetuate greater self-knowledge, understanding, and the inspired thoughts and desire to fuel our creative endeavors. Through our Sexual Self, we may tap into our natural ability to create loving relationships and embark on creative endeavors that manifest a life filled with love, abundance, and joy.

The healthy Sexual Self both seeds and nourishes that which is to become. The "outer layer" of the Sexual Self is the only part that is dependent on another individual to procreate, the physical form of our Sexual Self. The non-physical aspects of our Sexual Self are dependent upon our internal polar opposites – our male and female energies – and our awareness of their united purpose and the value of their cooperative power to create.

Our Male and Female Polarities

Each of us, no matter our physical gender, contains both male and female energy. In fact, this is true of ALL things. Both ancient philosophies, like the Hermetic philosophy described in the Kybalion, and modern science recognize that all things contain both masculine and feminine principles.

Our masculine energy is outgoing, "doing" oriented, expansive. It is the seeding factor, the directing force, the impetus that sends forth the seed of creative endeavor, that which is to be received. Our male aspect is the sperm of our thought seeking to unite with the feminine aspect or ovum of our feelings which nourishes our seed of thought. Our female energy is inward, inclusive, and creative. From its embryonic state to its perfect time of fruition, the female energy gives birth to the creative endeavors of our choice, then lovingly gives it back to the male aspect of our Sexual Self to successfully market and direct our creative endeavor into the world of form.

In science, the masculine energy is the "positive" and the female is the "negative." This is not to be confused with "good and bad." The male/positive and female/negative energy are simply the expression of the energetic movement of vibration – the male energy moving away from a central point and the female energy returning to a central point. This is vibration. Ancient wisdom has long maintained what science is now discovering — all things, including we human beings, are vibration. In other words, we are energy.

Our Sexual Self, as well as all our Selves, is influenced by where we are on our male/female polarity spectrum. If we are more in our male energy, we behave in more a "thinking and doing" way, direct, goal oriented, with little feeling. If we are in our female energy, we behave in a more "nurturing and feeling" way, flowing in creativity. If we are acting in male energy and our partner in male energy, collisions are likely to occur. ***Knowing the characteristics of male energy and female energy will help us understand our partner's behavior and more carefully choose our behavior in response.***

The ideal place to be on the male/female polarity spectrum is right in the middle, in that place where our male and female energies are balanced. You might say that this is a state of androgynous energy where both polarities, male and female, merge in a state of oneness to birth creative endeavors that benefit self and others. From this state, our Sexual Self is a creator, a self-contained aspect of us that births reality through experience.

The concept of God, Oneness, or Creator maintains that everything is contained within the One and everything that is created flows from the One. In that same way, we are created in the image of God/One/Creator in that we have within us the integral components of Oneness, wholeness, and the ability to create. Everything that is created in our life flows from ***within*** — the good, the bad and the indifferent. In other words, we are Gods birthing experiences for our Self -Realization. Until we understand our Sexual Self's role as Creator, we birth hellish experiences as haphazardly as we birth experiences of joy.

Fear of our Sexual Self, fear of our male/female energy, blocks our desire to create and freezes us in patterns of dull repetition rather than in patterns of successful creative endeavors. This includes our sexual life. Fear births feelings of resignation and falsely turns joy into a sense of duty. The Primal Force of Love, within our Sexual Self, is our greatest source to fuel our creative endeavors.

Alchemists at heart, we all create our daily lives and, through our many experiences, eventually gain wisdom. Unfortunately, many of our creative endeavors fail to fulfill our hopes and desires because of our narrow vision and unwillingness to move beyond our self-imposed restrictions. Our attempts to successfully create our hopes and dreams fall short of our expectations. We know that it takes two, a male and a female, to produce a baby. However, most of us do not know that it also takes both our male and female energy to fuel our greatest creative endeavors in all our Selves (which we will learn about in the next chapter), including the Sexual Self.

Once understood, fueling creative endeavors becomes a joy rather than a disappointment. Understanding the potentials of our Sexual Self is exciting. Fear of our Sexual Self is replaced with understanding its full and unlimited potential to fuel *all* our creative endeavors. Just imagine a never-ending creative flow of ideas taking form to benefit you and others. Fear is always our greatest enemy. Inspiration is always our greatest friend.

A COMMON MISTAKE IN RELATIONSHIPS

In marriage counseling, therapists often hear the same complaints. While the roles can sometimes be reversed, typically the wife complains that she feels used. When he wants sex, she is expected to be immediately ready, whether she feels like it or not. The husband complains that his wife never wants to have sex. In truth, our female energy within us, whether we are physically male or female, needs to feel love and affection to arouse desire. A clumsy hand on the breast and the statement, "Let's do it" rarely arouses desire. In this situation, the wife is completely turned off and her husband becomes confused. So many couples have stopped enjoying sensual, sexual relations because they do not know what is wrong. Both feel abused and used.

Men, particularly younger men, can think about sex and get an erection without any physical arousal activities. They can think it and do it. Action! The male energy within us all, whether we are physically a man or woman, thinks in this manner. As we noted earlier, our male energy is the source of our ability to direct and act. Some females have yet to develop their male nature. Others exclusively express it and have shut down their female aspect of feeling. On the other hand, some males have never developed their feminine nature. They are afraid of sensitivity, affection, and intimacy. Other males are afraid of their male energy and have difficulty moving past their emotional fears of rejection to pursue intimacy.

An understanding of our male and female energies is important to a healthy sex life. An understanding of one's own male and female energy is necessary to effectively communicate one's desires. The typical male partner, in his male energy feels aroused just by holding, being close to his partner. His male energy is ready to move fast, be directive. He immediately acts upon those feelings which comes out as "Let's do it." He has not learned how to relax and enjoy the female part of himself that enjoys cuddling and fondling without necessarily the physical act of sex. The typical female partner is aroused by loving, affectionate feelings, by feeling safe, valued, and loved. Female energy and true arousal will never come out if it feels trapped or overpowered by physical energy. Intimacy is important. Cuddling, teasing, taking one's time, allowing the love to flow between hearts – all these activities are a sure bet for full arousal, and enjoyable sex.

It is vital that we begin to open our awareness to our multi-dimensional Selves. There are so many benefits in practical ways of enriching our lives. We can explore our male and female natures with our partners if we are aware. We can discover new ways of fulfilling ourselves and our partners.

All healing begins with self-knowledge. We must choose love, peace, and joy to be in ultimate control of our lives. We must know ourselves enough to get a clear understanding of what we want and gain the confidence to pursue those things in a healthy way. The happiest relationships are those where both partners are aware of all aspects of Self. Neither partner is needy. Neither partner is dependent on the other. There is no competition, only the fullness of Self and an appreciation for the fullness of one's partner. One lifts the other, supports the other, and feels connected even when they are not physically together. Similarly, each can have "alone time" even when they are physically together. There is space and togetherness in their love. There is a oneness in their togetherness.

With a strong sense of Self, neither gets lost in the shadow of the other. They are partners because they choose to be partners – not for convenience, financial considerations, or duty. They treasure the loving feelings that flow between them. They do not compromise these feelings for the sake of "being right." They are considerate, thoughtful, and sensitive to each other's feelings. They care. They know their relationship is precious. Each are more powerful because of the love that flows between them. We cannot expect to have something we are not able to give. Finding the perfect man or woman is impossible until we are perfect. Ironically, we do not need perfection; rather we need the consistent heart-based living that attracts a partner with whom we can create a deep loving connection. Deep, loving connections transcend the need for perfection, recognizing and valuing the unique qualities of our partner.

ABANDONING THE FEMININE

It is common in today's world to forfeit our feminine energy. Here is the story of Brenda, whose fear kept her stuck in her male energy, preventing her from fully engaging her Sexual Self to fuel her most treasured creative endeavors.

Brenda was, by all social measures, an intelligent and successful person. Despite her outward success in life, she held deeply repressed feelings of being unworthy and physically unattractive. These feelings stemmed from her childhood. As an adult, Brenda consciously thought that she must use seduction and sex to obtain a relationship. She embarked on a series of intimate relationships that all resulted in disaster, leaving her in tears and adding a sense of failure to her feelings of unworthiness. Although she was not aware of this, Brenda saw that seduction did not get her what she wanted; she became afraid of the feminine aspect of her Sexual Self. As a result, Brenda made an unconscious decision to deny and desensitize her feelings for love because she believed she could no longer trust them.

Brenda began to rely solely on the male aspect of her Sexual Self to direct her life. She did everything herself, relied on no one, never asked for help. Her caring, loving, nurturing nature became so suppressed that she never exposed it during any activity of her life. Brenda wanted no one to interfere with her life. She isolated herself to such a degree she became cold and distant to old friends, was polite to her co-workers. She no longer engaged in any type of romantic friendships. Brenda became like a turtle withdrawn into her shell.

Brenda pushed herself to achieve with such force that her male aspect was exhausted. Her feminine aspect was not allowed to nurture her male for it had been forever banned from participating in her life. She believed that her feminine energy could not be trusted.

As you might imagine, Brenda's life did not improve. While Brenda was particularly good at maintaining what she considered her duties – work, social upkeep, paying the bills, and so on – the quality of her life continued to be cold, dull, and unfulfilling. There was a time when Brenda had many creative ideas; however, with her feminine energy so deeply repressed, creativity came to a halt. She was bored at work, at home and with herself. Television, take-out dinners, and thumbing through social media, became her friends. This lifestyle continued for quite a while. In this male energy, Brenda adopted an arrogant attitude to hide the emotional pain she was feeling.

Her attempts to feel better about herself and improve the quality of her life, instead of helping, set her on a downward spiral. First, Brenda decided that her happiness was dependent on finding a partner to help her in life. She was tired of coming home to an empty house, going to dinner or the movies by herself. How could she find a suitable partner when her only social interaction was at work? She did not understand why the males at her workplace ignored her. They were polite, but distant, when engaging in conversation with her. Brenda could not understand why they avoided her, especially since she had no romantic interest in any of them.

Brenda was unaware that energy never lies. She was unaware of just how withdrawn and bitter she had become. She looked in the mirror each morning but failed to see the distant look in her eyes or wrinkles in her frown, created from the many disappointments in life. Operating solely from her male energy, Brenda was tough and could manage being ignored. She further resolved that she did not need the approval of friends. Yet, Brenda was convinced that she needed a partner in her life. She was losing confidence in her ability to sustain her job, and she was bored with being by herself. Her creativity had dried up and Brenda hated the prune she saw when looking in the mirror. Tired of doing everything herself, she thought it was time for a mate, a male, to take care of her, but Prince Charming never showed up. She was at a loss about finding a mate.

At the height of her unhappiness, she cried and pleaded with God to help her get her life back. She did not want to die alone, nor *did she want to have a breakdown and let loose all that repressed unhappiness. That night, Brenda even had brief thoughts of taking her own life but became angry at herself when she realized she was too afraid to even do that. She did not understand how her life could have gotten to this stage of desperation. Why could she not find someone to take care of her needs emotionally and financially so she would not feel so much stress and tension? What did she do wrong? She hated herself and in desperation reached out to a distant God to help her find a life partner.*

The next morning, Brenda woke up with a smile on her face and a new glimmering light in her eyes. She looked forward to going to work, something she had not felt in an exceptionally long time. At work, Brenda noticed that her co-workers could feel the change in her. She was convinced that something of a miracle must have happened for her to feel so good.

Later that morning, her boss called her into his office where he offered her a promotion and a pay increase. Brenda was speechless. Her boss expressed his confidence in her ability to tackle her new responsibilities with ease. She was to assist the company's new attorney. Brenda was thrilled with this promotion and even more thrilled when her boss introduced her to Mark, the lawyer she would be assisting. Her eyes lit up the moment she saw him. "Oh my God," she thought "He is the most beautiful man I have ever seen." She could not believe these wonderful changes in her life.

As an attorney, Mark had an impressive portfolio of successful acquisitions. However, Brenda did not care about that. She was more impressed with his gentle, yet confident, manner and the caring quality she saw in his eyes. Mark showed Brenda her new office and indicated that they would undoubtedly be spending a lot of time together. She was thrilled and wondered how God could help her change her life that fast! She was so grateful and full of wonder; she was beaming with light and could not wait to begin her new position.

*In the days ahead, Brenda marveled at her good fortune. She just knew that God had presented her with a way to release her loneliness, boredom, and unhappiness. Her boss was always on her mind. He was so good looking and sexy – the perfect candidate for a life partner. "Slow down," she thought, "You do not even know him." Brenda concentrated on her work – rather she **tried** to concentrate on her work, but Mark WAS handsome and sexy. Mark was highly intelligent, hard-hitting, powerful in his demeanor with a sense of confidence and self-importance that confirmed itself each time he mediated an acquisition. Brenda could not help herself; she directed her thoughts towards getting her man. And she got him.*

Brenda and Mark married. She had attained her goal, having a partner to share in the responsibilities of life. However, after the "initial high" of their sexual experiences, Brenda did not feel the joy, fulfillment, and satisfaction she expected to feel. Nothing changed. Brenda continued to drive herself to the point of stress and physical breakdown. Mark continued to direct his thoughts solely towards acquisition. Both were functioning solely from their male aspects. What Brenda thought was the solution, brought momentary excitement but was not the long-term solution to her happiness.

Soon, Brenda felt more isolated than before. She observed Mark's less pleasant characteristics and habits – the condescending way he treated others, how he bended the rules to suit himself, how he manipulated discussions to his advantage, and how easily he could break trust because the end justified the means. Their sex life was non-existent, at best lifeless and boring. Brenda concluded that Mark's love could not be trusted. She examined their intimate time together and realized that he shares nothing of himself, shows no sense of genuinely caring, never talks about his feelings. Brenda wondered if Mark even knew what love is. As her situation began to dawn on her, she thought, "I am still alone and now I have a pompous ass telling me where to go, how to think, and what to do to be more successful!"

As you might expect, Brenda became resolved that all men are worthless, self-centered assholes. Once again, she returned to feeling nothing. Once again, her bitterness surfaced but she now directed that bitterness toward Mark as she promised herself that if he crosses her one more time, she will take him to the cleaners. Unhappy, she chose to stay in the relationship for convenience and appearances. Her male aspect was at its height, defenses up, always on guard, poised to win every argument.

Does this sound familiar? In this example, Brenda created an experience that was doomed to fail because she was functioning solely from her male energy, without an understanding of her female aspect and its importance in her life. She had denied her female aspect's participation in the creation of her experience with Mark because she did not trust or value the female aspect of her Sexual Self. So, instead of creating a sense of happiness, Brenda energized her long-repressed belief that she cannot trust love.

Brenda's thoughts and beliefs from her life experiences give her a very narrow view of life. She is not looking at the Big Picture. She thinks she is learning a lesson from her experience, but she is missing the message. Brenda must move beyond the outward appearance of events and look inward. She must go within and discover the creative abilities of her Sexual Self. By living and expressing from the fullness of her Sexual Self, including both her male and female aspects, Brenda will understand her life experiences more fully. She will be able to find creative solutions, to make centered decisions that break her pattern of engaging in unfulfilling relationships, and enable her to attract love, joy, and abundance.

So, what was happening with Brenda? In Brenda's early experiences, the shadow side of her feminine aspect was obvious. Unfortunately, she had not seen the light of her loving feminine power. Brenda was focused on the feelings of her lower desire body, persona and its delusions, and misused powers of seduction.

The shadow side of her feminine aspect created dark experiences, experiences that caused her to mistrust nature without ever experiencing the light of her loving power. Frightened of her own dark seductive powers and ability to create dark experiences, Brenda abandoned her feminine aspect and gave full power to her male aspect. She began expressing the light of her male nature by *taking action*. Because she lacked understanding of the light of her male nature, it was easy for her to slide into the shadow of her male nature, creating experiences of egoism and aggression. Cold and unfeeling, Brenda used brute force, producing, achieving, taking action, but allowing no time for relaxation and play, key elements required to replenish one's vital life force. As a result, she remained intensely stress and physically exhausted.

MISREADING THE MESSAGES

Without awareness of our Selves and our male/female energies, we misread our partner's verbal and non-verbal messages. In the above example, Brenda misread the lesson in this experience. As she reflected on her present situation and condition, she concluded that she did not want to experience life by herself. Still operating within her male energy, she determined that a partner would solve her problems. Once again, Brenda's male energy was jumping to solutions without considering, respecting, and valuing the feminine aspect. When unsuccessful,

Brenda even reached out to another "male" as defined by traditional religion – God.

Brenda's male aspect wanted a partner who was self-sufficient, financially abundant, and socially powerful. The energy of that thought manifested a male partner who exhibited all the characteristics she desired. Just like Brenda, her partner was living only within *his* male aspect and only expressing through the shadow side of his Sexual Self. Like Brenda he had not realized the light of his female side. As a result, Brenda experienced the coldness, the cruelty, the egotism and the aggression of his shadow male and the absence of his sensitivity, love, caring and nurturing qualities of his feminine aspect.

Brenda derived from this experience that she cannot trust men and that she is better off alone. Again, Brenda focused outward and never ventured inward to listen to the still small voice within that gently whispers the truth about her experiences and her Sexual Self.

If Brenda had ventured inward, she never would have abandoned her feminine aspect. She could have forgiven her temptress-like behavior and reined in her ability to get what she wants through seduction. She could have taken time to develop the light of her female aspect and enjoy nurturing the male aspect within her. She could have embraced the light of her male energy. The light of Brenda's thought, the male aspect, could have merged with the light of Brenda's feeling, the female aspect, to create experiences that would further develop and empower her Sexual Self.

Simply stated, fear caused Brenda's denial of her female energy which caused her shadow male to attract another shadow male. If Brenda had been in touch with her loving feelings, her intent would have been different. Her thought of having a partner would have merged with her desire to love another and be loved by another. Brenda would have manifested a healthy, balanced relationship of joy and love, stemming from her healthy and balanced Sexual Self. Fear can cause abandonment of the male aspect as well. Fear of one's own shadow male, and the egotism, aggression and brute force can inhibit our thought and directive ability to act. A person could be solely in the shadow or the light of female energy and experience lots of feelings, ideas, and dreams but never bring anything to fruition.

LIVING ON THE EXPRESSWAY OF LIFE

Most people travel through life on the Expressway where everyone is moving at breakneck speed. There is no time to stop and experience your feelings or why those feelings are there. Goodness! If you stop, you might be run over. You must keep up your pace, allow no one to pass – you must not trail behind. Do you feel the fear in those words? Those who live life on the Expressway experience constant stress, pressure, and anxiety. You must constantly keep your eyes on the road, no time to look around. When you do look around, you see signs, fields, cars, trucks, and interchanges. There is little to satisfy your sense of beauty. You might tell yourself that moving fastest, staying ahead, is worth it. But is it really? What have you given up? Why are you in such a rush?

Most of us are born on this broad highway. If we are lucky, we know our parents and family lineage. Whatever parents we get, we get. Many times, we feel different from our parents and family. When we are young, we greatly desire our parents' love and acceptance. Many times, love and acceptance are hard to attain. Sometimes parents want to change us, steer us in a direction that just does not express who we are. Sometimes parents want us to think and believe what they think and believe, leaving no room for difference or discussion. Sometimes our parents say they love us, but their actions say otherwise. Sometimes we can feel their love, even if they are unable to express it. Often as we mature, our parents still "see" us as little children.

We go to school and learn the curriculum of the day. We experience other events and activities outside our home. We see the Expressway. It is easy to feel ineffective and insignificant in such a big and fast-paced world. While each childhood brings its own "ups and downs," most of us grow up wishing we were different, had different hair, more clothes, a nicer body, more friends, different parents…the list goes on. Even me! I remember thinking I was the ugliest little girl alive. My arms were too big, and my hair was scrawny. I did not have many friends. My best friends were all my dogs. After school, I would go out in the dog pens and play for hours. The dogs accepted me as I was and loved me unconditionally, without waver. I could trust them to do that. I could not trust people to love me. I did not feel likable or lovable.

When we grow up and become what we understand to be responsible adults, we become the mothers and fathers. Many times, we work at jobs we do not like because it is all we are trained to do. Unfulfilled, we become burned out and wish our lives were different. Feeling trapped, we resign ourselves to this unfulfilled life and, often, we become angry about our lot in life. Many times, we become involved in a relationship or a marriage that is a pure pain in the neck. There is nothing easy about it. There is either control, abuse, indifference, anger, boredom, or other negative descriptions to explain what we thought would be a "live happily ever after" event.

Sometimes we feel like victims and quietly wonder what went wrong. We look at life as something that happens to us. Eventually youth wanes and we begin to worry about old age. If our parents had heart problems, cancer, or other hereditary diseases, we wonder if we will suffer the same because we have been told there is a good chance we will.

Things happen one after another. It seems we live many different lifetimes in one. Some segments we cannot remember at all and then, before you know it, we are at the end of life's journey. Not truly sure what happens after death, we want to believe what traditional religion purports – if we were good, we will go to heaven. Were we good enough? Sometimes it is easier to believe there is nothing after death rather than facing the scary prospect of being judged at the Pearly Gates. None of us particularly wants to go to hell; it has not received incredibly good reviews. If we do not fear death, most of us fear how we are going to die. We do not like what old age means or brings to us. The end becomes inevitable, and we do not even know what is next or if there is a next.

> *"There is more to life than increasing its speed."*
> ~Mahatma Gandhi

Our life is over before we know it, our bodies responding to our stressful and unfulfilling lives – bleeding ulcers, diabetes, arthritis, cancer, heart attack, Parkinson's Disease, dementia, the list goes on. Our life was moving so fast, we did not even sense the early symptoms. On top of that, we fear disease on The Expressway because it slows us down or stops us entirely. On the Expressway, it is too easy to become the victim of life, disease, or other people. No stopping to smell the roses. No stopping to catch your breath. No stopping to find that quiet place of repose within us. We look outward for answers, for self-worth, for purpose, for power. Having no boundaries, we put up with the constant criticism and advice of others. Having no understanding of self, we put up with our self-criticism and judgement.

We cannot control the world, but we do have a right to our own space. While we cannot be responsible for maintaining love and peace in the entire world, we can be responsible for maintaining our space with love and peace which, ironically, helps the entire world. We can enjoy our life and look forward to each day with enthusiasm and wander. Rather than living on the Expressway, we can choose an alternative lifestyle called The Path.

The Path to the Heart

There is an alternative to living life on the Expressway. There is a way to live a rewarding and fulfilling life. Sadly, many only choose the alternative when they have "broken down" on the Expressway, when circumstances force change, like a life-threatening illness, an ugly divorce, the death of a loved one, or old age. Such circumstances make it impossible to keep pace on the Expressway, requiring that they find another route. It is at these milestones that we are likely to begin our search for something different, more rewarding, healthier.

For example, someone overcoming a serious illness might explore healing through nutrition and alternative medicine therapies. Others may explore spiritual avenues or join support groups. It is often such life events that set us on "the Path," that is, the path to greater understanding of Self, of taking responsibility for improving the quality of life.

There are many reasons that movement on that fast-paced Expressway comes to a halt. When we are stopped, we can easily feel sorry for ourselves. We can lie down and just quit. We can slowly let our spirit drift far from our body until the vulture begins to circle. Or we can charge our spirit, fuel our love, and take responsibility for the life that flows through us. We can chart a new course, a course that no longer requires the Expressway.

We do not have to wait for a crisis to get off the Expressway. We can take responsibility for the quality of our life now. We can choose to have a healthy Sexual Self. We can choose an alternative lifestyle because we want love, joy, and greater abundance in our life. I have been on my Path for over fifty years. I developed my self-esteem and self-worth, recognized my qualities and talents, and understood my purpose in life using the processes and techniques described in this book. My greatest lesson learned from traveling my Path is this: If you ask from your heart, you will always receive.

On the Path to the Heart, one finds a creative free-flowing lifestyle, a lifestyle that makes it possible to discover Self, listen to the still small voice within our Inner Space, and begin to follow one's intuitive direction. There is time, all the time in the world, to discover new aspects and potentials of Self. There is more quality time to spend with loved ones and friends that you treasure. From this slower pace, one has time to acquire a deep appreciation for family, life, community, and giving.

> *Your vision will become clear only when you can look into your own heart. Who looks outside, dreams; who looks inside, awakes.*
>
> ~Carl Jung, founder of analytical

On the Path, there is time to enjoy nature which helps us feel a kinship with all life. Isolation depletes our energy and immune system, robbing us of our natural creativity and vitality. There is constant self-growth and progress, one step at a time. There is time to evaluate and appreciate the progress. There is time to be aware of our qualities and strengths and refine the areas we choose to improve. The Path provides space for taking care of Self and sorting out the "why" of difficult situations, so that we do not repeat negative experiences.

As I discovered Self, I faced the world with a healthy Sexual Self. In that healthy energy, I attracted the love of my life, Marshall Smith, and began a loving partnership of thirty-three years. We empowered the best in each other. Our healthy Sexual Selves enabled us to share the depth of ourselves, with love, confidence, and sheer joy. We were blessed.

Walking the Path is the ultimate adventure because one is moving toward the greatest prize, the full discovery of Self and the ability to live a joyful and fulfilling life that comes with a healthy Sexual Self. On this adventure of self-discovery, one can ask many questions and receive meaningful answers. Who are you? What is important to you? To what creative things are you drawn? What are you capable of accomplishing within the fullness of who you are? And, going even deeper, why are you on the Earth? What have you come to do? What happens when the physical body dies?

Walking the Path is about finding one's Self, one's purpose, and expressing these attributes in everyday activities. It is about love being more important than ambition. It is about exploring and expanding your potential, not keeping up with others. Walking the Path is about letting go of complaining and blaming, instead expressing one's goodness through the release of old negative habits and behavior. It is about living one day at a time, enjoying the beauty and harmony of the now, rather than planning every move from a limited vision full of fears. Walking the Path is about forgiving self for past mistakes, learning to love self, and finding peace with one's Self by letting go of judging and condemning self and others. It is about hope, faith, and trust rather than bitterness, cynicism, and hostility. It is about meaningful and satisfying sex on Saturday night.

Chapter Two:

—◆◆◆—

THE SEVEN MAJOR
ASPECTS OF SELF

"If there be righteousness in the heart, there will be beauty in the character.
If there be beauty in the character, there will be harmony in the home.
If there be harmony in the home, there will be order in the nation.
If there be order in the nation, there will be peace in the world."

~Confucius

THE BEST WAY of repairing one's relationship is healing one's Self. There is a well-known ancient Greek aphorism of "***know yourself***" that was interwoven throughout the philosophies of both Socrates and Plato. The *Aquarian Gospel* by Levi H. Dowling records the story of the disciples gathering around Jesus to ask questions. In this story, one disciple asked him, *"What is the most important thing we should know?"* to which Jesus answered, *"Know yourself."* The disciples, however, did not like that answer because it was not specific so they said, "*and what next* *should we know?"* Jesus answered once again, *"After you know yourselves, go back and know them some more."*

Knowing yourself means knowing who you are, your potential, the inherent abilities that lie with you. It also means discovering, understanding, and releasing those things that create limitation and dysfunction in your life. You cannot know yourself by looking in the mirror or by judging yourself for having a love affair, or by looking at your portfolio of investments. To know yourself means knowing all the aspects of yourself. It means knowing all the intricate, wondrous dimensions of yourself. We judge ourselves without knowing our Selves. We judge and compare then conclude we are failures when we have not been expressing our full abilities. We measure our abilities and our worth through our jobs, our homes, our hobbies, but really know very little about our true qualities and abilities.

SEVEN MAJOR SELVES AND YOUR SEXUAL SELF

So far, we have learned that the Sexual Self is more than physical sexual desire. The Sexual Self is a vibrant source of vitality and creativity. We have learned that the Sexual Self is affected by other aspects of our selves such as our male and female aspects. The Sexual Self is also affected by our seven major Selves, those key points from which energy flows. These Selves support our physical and emotional health. To fully understand our nature, our behaviors, and the influences around us, we must recognize ourselves as the multidimensional beings we are, possessing many aspects of Self.

Over the years, my research involved the recognition, function, and expression of the major aspects of Self, dissecting the whole being to find the parts that make up the whole. I began my research studying the seven major Selves in the physical body. There are numerous books written about them. Most of these information resources give the locations, color, sound frequency, and general function associated with each Self. While this was interesting, there was no material that helped me understand Self and *all* its aspects, especially these Selves as they relate to thoughts, feelings, and emotions. The Selves only began to have real significance to me when I began to develop the therapy process that came to be known as RoHun^{TM}. I realized that distinct personality traits, thought patterns, and feelings neatly corresponded with each Self. And, by working with our major Selves, we can realize the amazing, creative, and inspired individuals that we are.

Each of the seven major aspects of Self has a focus and energy just as each part of your physical body has a functional purpose. The hands, the feet, the liver, the heart, the eyes – each part of the body has a function. Each part of the body is important and must function in harmony. So, it is with your seven aspects of Self. Each aspect of Self has a name that describes its focus and function. The seven major Selves are:

- The Presence
- The Emotional Self, also called the Inner Child
- The Achiever Self
- The Loving Self
- The Creative Expressor
- The Intuitive Self, also called the Visionary
- The Angel

Each of our major Selves has its ways of understanding and processing our experiences. It is no wonder that we experience confusion about our thoughts, feelings, and behaviors. As we go inward and examine each of our major Selves, we will begin to see things more clearly. Clarity is a great gift. Going within brings clarity. When given tools to understand, one can progress in ways that are important to a healthy Sexual Self.

So, we are a complex group of Selves, each of whom have its unique focus and energy. Invariably, an interaction among Selves was behind the mistakes we have made as well as the catalyst for all our good deeds. To add to that complexity, the Sexual Self, just like all our Selves, impacts and is impacted by the seven major Selves.

We will learn about each major Self, its purpose and function and how each Self interacts with other Selves. We will start with the three most familiar and most troublesome aspects of Self – the Presence, the Emotional Self, and the Achiever – the three aspects of Self that developed in the early days of man's evolution. Of the seven major Selves, these three are of the lowest frequency and are home to the most dysfunctional thoughts.

THE PRESENCE

The Self called the Presence is located at the base of the spine. It is the Presence that the world sees – and what you see when you look in the mirror. It is the least refined and most ancient part of our Selves. Carl Jung, the great Austrian psychologist, called this aspect of Self, the Persona, or facade. This is what we show the world.

The Presence reflects the accumulation of one's thoughts and feelings about Self. It reflects an individual's self-image. The person with a low self-image Presence shies away from people, often looks downward a good bit of the time, and avoids eye contact. There is a lack of vitality in the eyes. On the other hand, when the Presence holds positive and healthy thoughts about Self, its energy flows outward and attracts like a magnet. In such cases, needs are satisfied without struggle. There is a popular expression, "You have to struggle to succeed" or "No pain, no gain?" Life is far from a struggle when one's Presence is confident, has high self-esteem, and positive thoughts and feelings. It may not always know how it will do something, but it knows it can. Thoughts are positive and therefore attract what the Presence desires rather than negative and resisting what it wants. Resistance attracts struggle.

When someone feels confident and abundant, his/her Presence exhibits higher thought and desires, so, naturally, that someone will attract situations and people who are of like higher thought and desires. One must feel abundant to attract abundance. Therein lies the importance of understanding one's self.

While a distinct and separate Self, the Presence represents all the other aspect of Self. It is one's ambassador and representative in the world. It reflects all other aspects of Self into the world. Are you familiar with your Presence? Are you aware of what you reflect to the world? Are you cognizant of the "You" that you outwardly present? Do you have a loving, confident, positive Presence? An arrogant, angry, and mean Presence? A shy, timid, mysterious Presence?

The unaware often do not understand the reactions they receive from other people. Speeding down the Expressway of life with little understanding of themselves, the unaware wonder why others are not engaging them in positive ways. Blaming themselves, the unaware reinforce and strengthen the negative thoughts and feelings about Self that are creating the challenges in the first place. It is easier to look outside one's self and blame others.

The Presence reflects all your Selves. As your Presence returns to full health, you will feel your beauty and youthfulness, a feeling that generates from within. You will find that your Sexual Self is more vibrant, creative, and full of vitality. Sex on Saturday night, both literally and figuratively, returns.

The Emotional Self, the Inner Child

"We can easily forgive a child who is afraid of the dark; the real tragedy of life is when adults are afraid of the light."

~Plato, Greek philosopher, ca. 400 B.C.

Here comes trouble! The Emotional Self, also called the Inner Child, is located just below the belly button. When healthy, the Emotional Self is responsible for one's vitality, youth, sensuality, and enthusiasm. Some think of this Self as a troublemaker. It can, in fact, cause many problems. In today's world, many of us stopped maturing emotionally around the age of ten. At around age ten, we acquire and solidify our negative thoughts and feelings about ourselves. It is also the time that we decide things like "I am not good enough," or "I am ugly," or "No one will ever love me." We develop behavior patterns, coping mechanisms, which mask any emotional pain we hold. We carry these coping mechanisms into adulthood — perhaps we are the office clown, or keep people emotionally distant, or are hermits in our homes.

The Emotional Self is also the place where desires are born, whether those desires are healthy or unhealthy. The Emotional Self wants what it wants when it wants. It may desire something, but it does not always have the means to fully understand the consequences of acting upon that desire. In fact, it just does not care about consequences. The Emotional Self wants. If it does not get what it wants, just like a child, the unaware Emotional Self will pout, scream, jump up and down, or seek revenge. Have you ever been out in public and noticed a child throwing a tantrum to manipulate its parent to get what it wants? The unhealthy Emotional Self behaves in this manner.

The Emotional Self is powerful. Here is a great example of the Emotional Self using the Sexual Self to get what it wants.

Beth is an attractive woman in her early thirties. For the most part, she feels good about herself and emits an aura of beauty and contentment. Lately, however, she has been feeling lonely. It has been several years since her divorce. So, Beth was hoping that she would meet someone special tonight at her friend's party.

By the time she arrives, the party is well underway. Everyone is eating, drinking, and socializing. Beth gets a drink and begins to mingle. Suddenly, out of the corner of her eye, she spots the most attractive man, a man with perfect hair, perfect body, perfect eyes. Beth feels her strong desire to be with this man. Her Emotional Self has energized her Sexual Self. Aroused, she is now on the prowl.

Without even knowing it, Beth draws the Lover energy from the collective conscious and becomes a goddess. Her skin becomes radiant, her smile sensual, her lips soften. She casually saunters over to the handsome man. When she speaks to him, she immediately envelops him in her goddess/Lover energy. He is now a god. He says and does exactly the right things. He is sensitive, loving, protective and has gentle strength. They are glued together. They talk all night. This perfect couple goes home together. What a perfect party! What a perfect night!

One year later, on a rainy evening, Beth is sobbing uncontrollably as she lay in her bed waiting for him to come home. He never came home that night. He was in the arms of another woman. Beth felt betrayed. She felt horribly used and painfully rejected. She threw him out of her life, but the damage to her heart was severe.

"I'll never let another man hurt me like that," she vowed, as she unconsciously placed psychic shields across her heart. She thought of her father and the trauma she experienced when, at age ten, her father left her mother for another woman. She never saw him again. "You can't trust any man," she cried into her pillow. "You can't trust love."

Was Beth really betrayed? Or did Beth's Emotional Self ambush her Sexual Self and take complete control of all other aspects of Self? Beth's Emotional Self wanted what it wanted when it wanted it. Beth's desire overpowered everything. She became a "goddess" to get what she wanted. The handsome man had little to do with the whole thing. He was simply caught in Beth's web.

If Beth could have sustained the goddess energy, the handsome man might have stayed in her web. But Beth is not a goddess. Her Emotional Self hijacked the energy to get what she wanted. The Emotional Self cannot sustain that intensity of desire. Eventually, the energy peters out, and the real person returns with all his or her grumpiness, personal habits, silliness, and aggravating coping mechanisms.

So, in Beth's case, all her quirks and bad habits came roaring back. All her partner's quirks and bad habits returned. Neither are perfect. The energy in the relationship dwindled. Her partner became unfaithful. Beth blamed her partner, her father, God, and, most of all, herself for being "stupid" enough to get involved. Beth was not stupid. She allowed herself to be controlled by her Emotional Self to get what she desired. She was deaf and blind to all else. Beth was unaware of her inner Selves and their imbalance and dysfunction. If Beth had been more aware of her Selves and all their components, the evening at the party might have unfolded like this:

Beth arrives at the party feeling good about herself and her life. She gets a drink and mingles with the guests. Out of the corner of her eye, she notices a very handsome man.

She thinks about approaching him but notices that he put his hand on a derriere of a pretty woman as she passed by him. The handsome man looks up. Their eyes meet. Beth can see that he is not ready for a meaningful relationship; he is only interested in having a good time without commitment. He was in a phase of needing to prove his worth to himself, and his behavior and energy reflected how it was still experimenting to find that self-esteem.

In this second scenario, Beth did not judge this man to be good or bad. She recognized from her clear observation where he was in his self-awareness and growth. Beth could admire and appreciate his handsomeness from afar or perhaps had a wonderful evening with him without the fantasy of a lifelong relationship.

So, Beth's partner did not betray her. At that time in his life, he was incapable of love or being faithful to one woman. Beth's desire blinded her objectivity. While the Emotional Self can be a troublemaker, when it is aware and behaves in healthy ways, the Emotional Self becomes a powerful force of healing and creativity.

Beth's story is typical and a great example of how, with the help of the Emotional Self, the Sexual Self can be overtaken. The Emotional Self's desire overpowers the Presence creating a physical desire for sex. When the Emotional Self compromises the Sexual Self to "capture" the attention and love of another, it always leads to trouble. Sexual desire is often misinterpreted as love. This weak foundation rarely, if ever, sustains a long-term, loving relationship. As it falls apart, partners in the relationship feel guilty, unworthy, and empty.

When led by an unhealthy Emotional Self, we tend to lose our higher faculty of wisdom. With a healthy Emotional Self, it is possible to make choices with greater clarity, to love ourselves, and even to have loving feelings for others without getting involved in sexual encounters with individuals about which we know little. If we shut off our emotions and our feelings, we are sacrificing a great aspect of ourselves. Shutting down is not the answer.

WOUNDED INNER CHILD

An unhealthy Emotional Self invariably has a wounded Inner Child lying deep in caverns of hurt and misbelief. When the Inner Child is healthy, mature, and understands that it is not abandoned, the Emotional Self becomes a positive and powerful force. It becomes the healer of the physical body. It gives one the desire and vitality to get up in the morning, to participate in the day, to be involved with one's partner.

If the Inner Child is emotionally wounded, we become afraid of our emotions and feelings. We have no desire to be in touch with our feelings because our feelings about ourselves and our life are unpleasant. When we shut down our emotions, we begin to dry up. We lose our vitality. Everything becomes duty. Everything becomes routine. We lose that sense of awe, that spark, that juice that makes us feel vitally alive.

Given our instinctual need to feel and be with others, and for our own emotional health, we must be able to make safe connections with other people. We must have "juice" going back and forth with others. We must dare to care again.

How does that Inner Child reach the point of shutting down? Imagine this scenario:

> *Mary, a ten-year-old child, sits on the back steps of her house looking sullen and staring into space. She has just had a horrendous fight with her brother. She sits alone, feels alone. At this moment, she has severed emotional ties with her brother, and with her mother for supporting her brother in the argument, with her father for being married to her mother, and with her friends for never being there when she needed them. Mary is experiencing a total state of isolation.*

If you could read this young girl's thoughts, you would hear words like these repeating themselves like a tape recorder in a never-ending loop — "No one understands me, and no one cares." Mary's perception at that moment is truth to her. No one cares, no one understands, I am alone. These embedded thoughts alter her perception of Self and her world. She believes she is isolated. This part of her never really participates in life. She becomes disconnected from life itself.

Will Mary ever recover? We know that Mary will eventually get off the back steps, go inside her home, play with her brother and her friends, and kiss her mother and father goodnight. Yet even though she participates in these routine events in her life, she now has a new façade, her Presence enables her to go through the motions, and the Emotional Self shields and protects that wounded little girl. Behind this façade, those negative thoughts still vibrate, while Mary silently and unconsciously resolves that no one will ever hurt her again, others do not matter, and she can play the game of life. Mary's story continues:

Mary's mind and body matures. She leaves home, gets a job, marries, and has children of her own. Her daily life is hectic. Responsibilities as an employee, wife, and mother consume all her time. There is not a moment to think of herself. Mary is constantly doing for her family, her work, and others. She falls into bed at night tired and already thinking of tomorrow's tasks and duties.

Mary's husband is a good man. He is supportive, thoughtful, and a good provider. As time goes by, her children grow up and have left home. All outward appearances indicate a happy and fulfilled life. Yet, at one o'clock in the morning, when all is quiet, tears slowly fall down her face. Mary feels terribly alone. Even with her husband sleeping soundly beside her, she feels isolated, apart from everything and everyone.

What is happening to Mary? With grown children, Mary's duties as a mother have shifted and no longer require so much of her time, leaving her feeling restless and empty. Her job has ceased to be stimulating. Every day is just a repetitious dull routine. Mary is tired and feeling old. Life no longer holds anything of interest to her. The tears continue to trickle down her cheeks. Deep within her, that wounded child who was locked away for decades, hidden from harm's way, is sobbing violently.

No longer distracted by responsibilities and duties, Mary's façade of protection weakens. Her Inner Child, the young girl who believed she was different, misunderstood, and alone, has stepped out of her internal hiding place and, as a result, Mary feels her sadness, unhappiness, and aloneness. In these moments, when the repressed thoughts of the Inner Child surface, one cannot help but feel the emotions, even though one is not consciously aware of its source. In Mary's case, she gets up from a night of tears, goes to work depressed, deeply aware of her isolation.

Mary's story continues:

> *Days pass. Weeks pass. Her husband finally notices that something is wrong. He suggests she go to the doctor to get something, some medication, for her depression. Mary resists every suggestion that her family or friends offer, all the while thinking, "They do not understand. I am alone." Of course, these thoughts take her into deeper feelings of isolation while a silent rage begins to form waves of hostile and resentful feelings. Marys' Inner Child is now angry at everyone, at life, at God, at all humanity for never being there for her. In between the bouts of anger, Mary becomes sad, a sadness that she is unable to talk about with anyone. Mary just knows that no one cares, no one understands. How could she and why should she talk to anyone?*

Two years later, her marriage is near divorce, her children are busy with their lives, and she has left her job for health reasons, embarrassing bladder problems. Mary gains twenty pounds. Soon she begins having nagging lower back pains. She rarely feels good and seldom has the energy to move through her day. Mary is 48 years old but feels like a 70-year-old.

Sitting in her kitchen one morning, Mary realized that she just did not have the energy to go through the day. Her heart was not in it. She saw no joy and had no interest. Yet, suicide was not an option for her. Mary was facing the longest day of her life. Her husband was working late, she languished in this feeling of despair and aloneness. By early evening, Mary not only gave up hope for something better, but she also gave up faith that her life would ever be meaningful. Those dark glooming thoughts from her Inner Child consumed her. Mary could no longer feel love, even the love of her family. She turned inward, giving in completely to the Inner Child's harsh thoughts. It was at that moment, her spirit, the spark of light and love within her heart, the source of her life force, began to separate from her body to seek another form that would express its purpose. Two months later, she was diagnosed with cancer and was told she was terminally ill. Six months later, she died at the age of fifty.

At Mary's funeral, her family and friends cried as they remembered her as a good person, someone who always did for others.

What happened to Mary? She never knew that the perception of life she developed when she was a ten-year-old child would affect her later life. Mary never became aware of the source of her profound sadness, isolation, and anger. The façade of protection she created worked for a while, but not forever. She succumbed to the emotional wounds of her childhood without ever being aware that her issues were coming from deep within her.

Our Inner Child is a precious life-giving, awe-inspiring part of us that, when allowed to mature and express, provides for our eternal youth, supplies the vitality and spontaneity needed to live healthy and happy life. It requires love and emotional nourishment to thrive. Yet, many people grow up in dysfunctional families and many of us carry the deeply repressed thoughts and faulty perceptions of a wounded Inner Child. For a time, we can muffle the feelings of isolation, sadness, abandonment, disappointment, or distrust, but eventually those perceptions will surface and create problems.

Know that this Inner Child can be rescued and healed. A healthy Inner Child within our Emotional Self can be a healing force, providing exuberant energy to live an inspired and creative life. As will all our Selves, our Emotional Self and Inner Child are worthy of our love.

THE ACHIEVER

> *"Your reason and your passion are the rudder and the sails of your seafaring soul. If either your sails or your rudder be broken, you can but toss and drift, or else be held at a standstill in mid-seas. For reason, ruling alone, is a force confining; and passion, unattended, is a flame that burns to its own destruction. Therefore, let your soul exalt your reason to the height of passion, that it may sing; and let it direct your passion with reason, that your passion may live through its own daily resurrection, and like the phoenix rise above its own ashes."*
>
> **~Khalil Gibran, Lebanese American writer, poet, and visual artist, 1883-1931**

We live in an achievement-oriented world. We judge and are judged many times by what we possess or what we have accomplished. We have become a society that believes individuals ARE what they do. If we do not achieve, we are nothing. Many people believe and live as if their thinking mind is everything. However, the Achiever, our mental body, our ability to reason and analyze, is only one-seventh of our vital functions. We are not what we do. We are who we are. ***The Achiever is simply that part of us that "does."*** Located just above the belly button, the Achiever is an extraordinarily strong Self.

When the Achiever is immature, disconnected, and unaware of the other aspects of Self, it takes on an air of self-importance. The thoughts and feelings housed within this Self become haughty, manipulative, and controlling. Our accomplishments become all important and of more value than our connection with people, especially our loving relationships. The Achiever, in its zealous quest for recognition and acknowledgment, moves further away from other Selves, like the Loving Self, who could keep it in check. Alone, the Achiever can be relentless and ruthless. It can all too easily follow that Machiavellian philosophy "the end justifies the means." At its worst, immature and without balance from the Loving Self, the Achiever will seek to overpower and control, even at the sacrifice of all other Selves. Happiness, peace of mind, love, and health means very little in comparison to achievement.

On the other hand, when the Achiever is aware, it respects and values the functions and abilities of the other six Selves. The aware Achiever accomplishes more with less effort. Liken it to a successful and winning sports team. A team that respects and values its members knows how to utilize the strengths of each of its members. They are in alignment. Each member steps up at the exact best moment to move the team forward. Together they achieve, together they win. Every member is rewarded. Each is recognized. They are a well-functioning team.

Sadly, not all teams are aligned, especially with the lower three Selves. When disharmony or disrespect occurs, the scores suffer. When the Achiever seeks control or dominance, it loses awareness of its "team," the other Selves – or creates a war among the Selves, causing tremendous frustration and internal conflict. Here is a good example:

In her early thirties, Barbara was diagnosed with diabetes. She was instructed to take medication and change her diet to keep her blood sugar levels within healthy ranges. The doctor was very candid with her when he warned that if she did not change her diet, she would soon be on insulin. He also told Barbara of the dire consequences of diabetes left untreated — blindness, loss of limbs, and early death. She panicked. She made resolutions to change her diet immediately.

Barbara had a high level of stress in many areas of her life. Her Achiever was in high gear. Running her own printing business, she worked long hours often under pressure of meeting tight deadlines. In addition, Barbara had three teenage children, two daughters and a son. A single parent without any support, coping with all the daily tasks that required her attention, she would grab lunch at a fast-food restaurant and snack throughout the day. Dinner depended on what the children's extra-curricular activities were that evening. There were no planned, routine meals except on Sunday. Barbara loved to bake, so, when she had time on Sunday, she often made pies and cakes which were usually eaten by Sunday night.

So, when Barbara learned she had diabetes, her Achiever made the resolution to change her eating habits. The reasons are good. She has three children to raise by herself. She made a plan – a plan she resolved to stick to no matter what.

Well, by the end of the first week, she had not followed her plan at all. Her Emotional Self did not allow it. She just had to have that brownie snack. She could not make cakes and pies without eating them. Her Emotional Self ate more than it had ever eaten, just to show her who was boss. She would die without the brownie, and she will die with them.

Barbara's Achiever made resolutions. It had a plan. But her Achiever and Emotional Self were not functioning as a team. To continue the sports analogy, the Emotional Self kept slipping the ball past the goal-keeper, so to speak. The Emotional Self wins, the Achiever loses, while the Presence becomes more confused, feels more out of control and helpless, like a true victim. Victim of who or what? Victim of self.

Wait a minute! Barbara's Selves are supposed to be on the same team. What happened?

Unless the Selves are working together, the mission will never be accomplished. The Emotional Self will always ignore the Achiever. As we noted earlier in this chapter, the unhealthy Emotional Self has the intensity, vitality, and power to get what it wants – even if what it wants is unhealthy for the entire energy system.

Unfortunately, because of societal pressure to achieve, most of us have attached our self-worth to achievement and must achieve to feel any sense of worth. To do this, we allow our Achiever to dominate, caging our Emotional Self in our dungeon of repressed thoughts and throwing away the key. The Achiever becomes convinced that it cannot trust the Emotional Self, counting all the times that the Emotional Self caused problems. The Achiever strengthens its determination by fueling the misguided thought "Every time I feel, I get hurt."

Individuals whose Achiever dominates have given up their ability to feel to maintain control, to prevent problems. In these cases, the Emotional Self is not dead. It waits and watches for the opportunity to seek revenge. When the Achiever is in charge, life is work, work, work. The Achiever would rather be doing than feeling. It feels its self-worth only through doing. Sadly, it is possible to work yourself to death. Our

Achiever, our mental body, can drive us to a state of physical illness. The Presence cannot keep up the same pace as the Achiever. Eventually, the Presence's etheric body breaks down, causing our physical body to break down. We get sick.

Unfortunately, most people are unaware of their higher Selves. So, when they get sick, not realizing there are alternatives, they drop into the energy of the Emotional Self. That Emotional Self, that Inner Child, has been locked in a cage with no opportunity to play or even be heard. It has spent its time being angry or feeling sorry for itself. It has been suffering and now its sweet revenge is becoming the victim, complaining about everything and everyone.

"No one calls me when I'm sick". *"I care about others. Why can't they be thoughtful?"* Whine, whine, whine! Everything is wrong and there is something wrong with just about everyone. We are miserable. Believing that there are no good feelings anywhere, we fuel the thought, *"I'm not going to care about anyone anymore."* Poor me.

Despite the misery, the individuals with strong Achievers force themselves to get well. They put their nagging, whining, angry Emotional Self back in the cage and let the Achiever dominate again, losing themselves in doing to avoid feeling.

BURN-OUT AND ILLNESS

As you have discerned by now, the Achiever is not a "feeling" aspect of Self. Its purpose is to reason and accomplish. Our achievement is our testimony to worth – to our self and to the outside world. We start to feel better about ourselves. Through behavioral conditioning we find this is a safe dimension of Self. We value ourselves more highly when we are worth something.

When we are always doing, we leave little time for anything else. There is no time for relaxation, for the personal needs. There is no time for family outside the context of doing. We "do" at work and come home only to continuing "doing." This is a destructive spiral. The body burns out. Tired, we lose our patience with others. We become hard-hearted. Caring takes time away from "doing." Being loving and sensitive only gets in the way of getting things done. We have every excuse in the world to justify our hard-heartedness. We are deeply embedded in the misbelief that actions do not hurt us, people hurt us. Therefore, doing is safer and more constructive. We stop expressing from other aspects of Self and only produce from our mental body, our Achiever. But eventually, the Achiever becomes dissatisfied. At some point, we get very tired. Everything becomes an effort. We feel as if we are pushing our way through life, forcing ourselves to get things accomplished.

When we let our guard down for an instant, the negative weight we are carrying, squeezes through the bars of our cage. We feel depressed, stuck, and burned out. What we once loved and enjoyed is no longer fulfilling. The vitality of our Inner Child, our Emotional Self, is diminished, leaving only aggravation, anger, and dissatisfaction. So, now, both the Achiever and the Emotional Self are unhappy. When this happens, the Presence does not know what to do. It too is tired and has little of the physical energy it once had. The Achiever and Emotional Self are using up all its energy.

At this point, the Presence feels trapped. Thoughts begin to swirl, "I cannot get another job. I am too old. I have no other skills. What if I become financially strapped? Oh, I cannot change jobs." In all this confusion, the Presence cannot see a solution, a way out of its situation.

When the Presence feels trapped and confused, the Achiever, in its efforts to feel better, does what it does best – it isolates. The Achiever takes its stalwart stance, saying to itself, "I must do everything myself if I want it done right." When our Achiever is in this space, we come righteous.

We perceive everything as either right or wrong according to our own values. Being right becomes more important than making it work – even with our loved ones. And, in this space, our Sexual Self and our loving relationships suffer. We forget that we once fell in love with our spouse just the way they are. Now, we attempt to create them in our image according to who we think they should be and what we think they should be doing. We become their unsolicited teachers, coaches, managers, and manipulators. We are no longer a loving spouse, friend, and supporter We become the enemy, watching for weakness and mistakes, and take pride in our ability to analyze what is wrong with them.

We view our children as our possessions. We strive to create them in our image according to the gospel of our Achiever. They must accomplish what we think is right for them giving no credence to their strengths, talents, character, or desires. This approach with our children creates disharmony and wounds that child's Emotional Self – this perpetuating the cycle of dysfunctional and poor emotional health. According to the Center for Disease Control, using data from 1999 through 2006, suicides were 11 percent of all deaths among teenagers. Parenting solely from the Achiever has little, if any, benefit. If the Achiever exclusively directs your life and the lives of others, it is time to re-evaluate.

Our Presence, Emotional Self, and Achiever are essential parts of our key seven Selves. And, as you can see, they interact closely with each other. If the Emotional Self and Achiever are dysfunctional, it is only a matter of time before the Presence, too, becomes unhealthy. Negative thoughts and negativity, in general, prevail. In that energy, we perceive everything we experience as being negative.

Yes, our Achiever is an expert at accomplishment. However, its purpose does not lie solely in achievement and the acquisition of material trophies. Our Achiever can move mountains when inspired by the next higher dimension of Self.

"Though I speak with the tongues of men and angels, and have not love, I am become as sounding brass, or a tinkling cymbal. And though I have the gift of prophecy, and understand all mysteries, and all knowledge; and though I have all faith, so that I could remove mountains, and have not love, I am nothing. And though I bestow all my goods to feed the poor, and though I give my body to be burned, and have not love, it profiteth me nothing. Love suffereth long, and it is kind, love envieth not; love vaunteth not itself, is not puffed up. Doth not behave itself unseemly, seeketh not her own, is not easily provoked, thinketh no evil. Rejoiceth not in iniquity, but rejoiceth in the truth; Beareth all things, believeth all things, hopeth all things, endureth all things. Love never faileth."

~ 1 Corinthians 13:1-6

Midway among our Selves, the Loving Self is a key influencer for all the other Selves. The awakened Loving Self is the conductor in this symphony of Selves. In an emotionally healthy individual, the lower Selves work in cooperation with the Loving Self and the higher Selves become instruments of the Heart. So, what is this Loving Self?

The Loving Self is located at the sternum, in the general area of the heart. Like other Selves, Loving Self can become unhealthy, dysfunctional, filled with faulty thoughts concerning love. Common faulty thoughts in this Self include, "You cannot trust love" and "Everyone you love leaves you." You might think that these thoughts would be stored within the Emotional Self. However, throughout our life, after repeated failed relationships, we can begin to blame love rather than our overzealous desire to get what we wanted.

Most people love from their Emotional Self. This is conditional love.

For example, some parents love their children with the unspoken thought, "I love you as long as you are a good reflection of me," or "If I cannot handle what you do and who you are, I do not want to be involved with you because I cannot handle the pain you cause me." Similarly, spouses who only have conditional love for their partners may think and feel, "I love you only if you are mine. If you leave me for any reason, I hate you. I hope you burn in hell." Emotional love can be possessive, jealous, manipulative, and vengeful if it does not get its way. Our Emotional Self wants its way all the time and its capacity to love is always conditional. Conditional love usually stems from deeply rooted thoughts and feelings of hurt and pain.

The Loving Self is that part of us who cares, who has compassion for others, who recognizes, acknowledges, and values that we each have our unique characteristics. The Loving Self is the source of unconditional love. But remember, it is unconditional love that enables us to set boundaries, to understand what is acceptable for a safe and healthy relationship, and to find the strength to say "no" when necessary.

The Loving Self, like its counterparts, can become unhealthy. At these times, we can develop Heart Quakes and Heart Dungeons.

HEART QUAKES

The sadness and pain we feel in our heart comes from some of the thoughts and feelings that are lying on the surface of our Loving Self. Our feelings of futility and thoughts of hopelessness cause what I like to call heart quakes. A Heart Quake shakes away our positive thoughts, leaving thoughts of harsh self-judgement and little worth. For the most part, these thoughts are deeply repressed and, while we might be unaware of them, we are still very much affected by them. With Heart Quakes, we exaggerate our shortcomings and perceive every tiny mistake as an unforgivable deed. Those who feel they are no damn good are in a Heart Quake. Those who are afraid to let another person get close are in a Heart Quake.

In these situations, our heart is not dead. Our heart is not the dark clouds of thoughts that hover over us. Our heart cannot be extinguished by our thoughts. Love is our true nature; the depth of our love is who we really are. The Loving Self waits to be recovered and set free. The Loving Self always waits, no matter how long it takes, for us to acknowledge it. The Loving Self waits to be freed to create love and abundance in our life.

In Jean Houston's book, *The Search for the Beloved*, she speaks about the sacred wound.

> *"Sacred Psychology is the process and practice of soulmaking; and soulmaking, as you may have discovered, is not necessarily a happy thing. Critical parts of it are not. As seed-making begins with the wounding of the ovum by the sperm, so does soulmaking begin with the wounding of the psyche by the Larger Story.*
>
> *Soulmaking requires that you die to one story to be reborn to a larger one. A renaissance, a rebirth, occurs not just because there Is a rising of ancient and archetypal symbols. A renaissance happens because the soul is breached. In this wounding, the psyche is opened, and new questions begin to be asked about who we withdrawal but can lead to the seeding of the world with the newly released powers of the psyche. A larger story is revealed by the wounding. When psychological energy is no longer bonded to social forms then uncensored, depth images and archetypes can have their day. Whether they serve to madden or illumine are in our depths. These powerful questions need not lead to alienation and is up to us.*
>
> *The classical Renaissance was a golden time when internal and external realities flowered together. The internal world knew the*

cosmos for its own, and the external world became "psyche-tized."
The spillover of psyche's abundance into the outer world primed the
creation of vital and resonant arts, sciences, history, statecraft, and
philosophy.

So, too, is your wounding, the breaching of your soul, an invitation
to your renaissance. Our wounding tells us that old forms are ready
to die, however reluctant the local self may be to allow this to occur,
and that hither-to unsuspected new forms are ready to flower.

As the "ties that bind" loosen in our culture and in our psyche,
the incidence of wounding accelerates and comes in many guises.
Consider your physical wounding: illnesses, accidents, birth, or ge-
netic defects. Consider the acts of violation upon your person: rape,
incest, child abuse, torture, robbery. Consider the losses you have
endured: the loss of a deep relationship, the loss of a job, the loss of a
marriage, the loss of sanity, the loss of self-esteem, the loss of status,
the loss of financial security. Consider those Soundings that have
afflicted cultures and nations: famine, plague, enslavement, war.
The list seems endless.

Wounding involves a painful excursion into pathos, wherein the
anguish is enormous, and the suffering cracks the boundaries of
what you thought you could bear. And yet, the wounding pathos
of your own local story may contain the seeds of healing and trans-
formation. The recognition of this truth is not new. In the Greek
tragedies, the gods force themselves into human consciousness at the
time of pathos. It is only at this time of wounding that the protago-
nist grows into a larger sense of what life is all about and can act
accordingly.

The wounding becomes sacred when we are willing to release our
old stories and to become the vehicles through which the new story

may emerge into time. When we fail to do this, we tend to repeat the same old story repeatedly. If you have a neurosis or psychosis, it probably originated in pathos that was not to its source in a Larger Story. If we would only look far enough, we would find that our wounding has archetypal power. In uncovering their mythic base, we are challenged to a deeper life. As Carl Jung has reminded us, it makes a difference whether we serve a "mania" which is detestable and undignified, or a god, which is full of meaning."

Sandra Castellucci wrote an article, published in Delphi University's *Healing Arts Journal 1977*, a true story that so eloquently describes the effects of heart quakes. She wrote:

"David was a Navaho Indian born on the reservation. By the time he was fourteen, he was an alcoholic. At 15, he and a friend of his, another Navaho, ran away from the reservation and joined the Merchant Marines. They met up with another runaway - a German boy, and they all became fast friends, and shipped all over the world together.

David was an artist, and, as they traveled, he would sketch the things he saw. What he did not know was that the things he was sketching were Japanese bunkers which were being prepared prior to the beginning of World War II. He submitted his sketches to the American military, and later enlisted in the military service. He thought he would continue to be an artist for the military, but the military, instead, made him a decoder. Navaho was the one language that the Germans did not know. They did not have any Navaho in Germany. They thought it was a code and could not break it. It used symbols, and different intonations at different times. It became the unbreakable code used during the war.

David was dropped behind enemy lines to do his job as a decoder.

Later, he was captured by the Germans, and was tortured unmercifully. They nailed his feet to the floor and made him stand there for three days. He was beaten repeatedly, and much more. The Germans then determined that he was not worthy to keep alive - he was a third-class citizen anyway, just an Indian, so they sent him off to Auschwitz, to the death camp. He was being shuffled off to the cattle car, and there was a German soldier with a rifle jammed into his back, shouting at him. Well, the soldier friend pulled him out of the crowd and made other arrangements for him to be sent to another camp.

At this camp, David was by then so ill and broken that all he could do was lie on a bunk in a stupor. Every day one German guard would come by and push maggots into his mouth, or chicken gizzards, and David was too weak to stop him. Well, the war dragged on, and then finally ended. When the Americans came to liberate the camp, and questioned David, he replied in Russian, perfect Russian. He somehow was channeling Russian and had no memory of American language. He was released to the Russians, who rejected him as not theirs, sent him back to the Americans, and he ended up at last, somehow, at the Veteran's Hospital in Battle Creek, Michigan, USA. He lapsed into a coma for two years. After he awakened, he could not walk - he was a cripple, and used braces on his legs and crutches to drag himself around.

He determined at that time to return to his tribe, make peace with them, and then return to the Veteran's Hospital to live out the time that was left to him before he died. So, he went home, and when the tribal elders saw and talked to him, they called a council meeting to discuss how they would help him. They took David, tied a rope around his waist, threw him into deep water, and told him, "Call back your spirit, David. You have no spirit. Your spirit is still in Germany. Call it back!" Well, David said calling his spirit was harder to do than standing for three days with his feet nailed to the floor. To call back his spirit, he had to go through every trauma he had lived through in the war. He saw the faces of all his tormentors, and he had to release them, forgive them, and let them go. And when the face of the guard that had come every day and fed him maggots and chicken gizzards appeared before him, he said, "OK, I don't know why you did it, but I release you, I forgive you." As soon as David did that, the face of the guard turned to him and said, "I did it to keep you alive, David, it was the only food I could find." And then it disappeared. By releasing and forgiving the guard, David was able to open to the bigger purpose that he had not been able to see before. David's spirit returned, he taught himself to walk again, and went on to become a shaman, a medicine man, and was an instrumental force in his tribe's life.

Note: Many years later, in December, he called a friend of his, an editor, and said, "Hi Carolyn, how are you doing?" Carolyn replied, "Fine David, what are you doing here (this city)? David said, "Oh nothing - just passing through. I just wanted to ask you if you would publish my biography for me?" She thought it strange that he said biography, but not everyone was as fussy as editors about the proper terminology, so she said, "Sure David, I'd love to publish your biography." David thanked her and ended the conversation, and she did not think any more about it.

In December, another friend called her and asked if she knew that David Paladin had died on December 18th. David had called her from the beyond to ask a favor of her, but nothing happened for several years. Then one day, an editor friend of hers called her and said "Carolyn, I'm editing a collection of stories about people, and I wondered if you would edit the story about David Paladin, since you knew him personally?" And she performed the favor asked of her by David Chet La Hey Paladin so long before."

HEART DUNGEONS

In addition to heart quakes, there are heart dungeons. Heart dungeons are formed by self-hatred, those ugly beliefs that we are evil. It is the place where we are forever judging our past wrong deeds and abuse of power. These are the thoughts that form the ugly scenes, the frightening feelings, and the fear that convinces us that we are heartless and do not deserve the good things in life. These negative thoughts of Self form the dungeons designed to trap our so-called demons that we fear are within us.

> "The only devils in the world are those running in our own hearts. That is where the battle should be fought."
>
> ~Mahatma Gandhi

When we harbor these types of thoughts, we feel we are living a lie. We feel phony. We create facades to fool people, but we can never let anyone close for fear they find out how despicable we are. We have eternally damned ourselves because of our wrong doings. We have determined that we do not deserve happiness, abundance, or even good luck. Like a recurring tape, we repeatedly tell that feeling good will always be followed by feeling bad. That tape eternally assures us that if anyone ever knew the "real" us, they would not like us. On and on, every day, every hour, every minute, that tape creates a hell within us, hells of our own making, hells that our thoughts create, not our wrong doings.

Most of the time, our thoughts of self are far worse than anything we have ever done. We hold ourselves back from positions of leadership because we do not trust ourselves. We are afraid of our power. We are afraid we will abuse it. We feel unworthy as if something deep inside us tells us we are undeserving. While sometimes these fears of Self are conscious, more times than not, they are unconscious, occasionally leaking

SEX ON SATURDAY NIGHT

into our lives like a poisonous gas, crippling us just when something important or wonderful is about to happen. Of course, we think that these horrible thoughts must be true or else we would not have them. It never occurs to us that these negative thoughts and feelings are the result of self-condemnation and our own lack of awareness and inability to forgive ourselves.

Our Loving Self has the power to break down the walls of the heart dungeon, to remove the armor created by heart quakes, to send the so-called demons to the Light. The Loving Self has the capacity to forgive our Selves and others for any injuries. We can resurrect our heart, restore our Loving Self to its full nature, and start over. Our Loving Self is the primal force of all good and abundance.

THE HEALTHY LOVING SELF

Forgiveness is the key to a healthy Loving Self, forgiving all known and unknown errors in judgment, mistakes, and wrong doings, perceived or real. To forgive others, one much first forgive one's Self. To love and value others, one must first love and value one's self. Although heart quakes and dungeons squelch all loving feelings towards Self, you can move the debris aside, become aware of some of the treasures of your heart, then begin to heal those things that created the heart quakes and dungeons. Experiencing the power of your Loving Self gives you the strength, will, and courage to forgive Self for your unawareness and release the debris that was covering the expression of your love. You can begin to create a loving, fulfilling life.

HEARTSONGS

Have you heard the phrase "song in your heart?" When you feel an intense, euphoric feeling of joy and contentment, you are feeling that song in your heart. It is the healthy Loving Self's way of rejoicing in life.

P. J. Skerrett, in an article published in the March 1997 issue of Popular Science magazine, wrote:

> *"A song in your heart may do more than boost your spirits - it may also signal a healthy ticker. While it may feel like your heart has the steady beat of a ticking metronome, there is a lot of variation in the time between one heartbeat and the next. At first glance, the intervals appear to be random. But to Harvard Medical school cardiologist, Dr. Ary Goldberger, there is some order in the randomness that tells an important story. Healthy hearts, it turns out, have more beat-to-beat variability than ailing hearts.*
>
> *They also have an inherent song. After making hours-long heartbeat recordings of volunteers' hearts, Goldberger and his associates averaged the intervals of every 300 beats (to smooth out changes caused by moving or breathing) and mapped the resulting whole numbers to notes on the diatonic scale. What the researchers expected was random noise. What they got instead was often quite musical, with the recordings from healthy hearts yielding more interesting melodies than those from disease-damaged hearts.*
>
> *Goldberger's son, pianist, and composer, Zach Davids, added rhythm and harmonies to these natural melodies and recorded them for a CD called Heartsongs. The songs sound much like a jazz or New Age composer noodling around at the keyboard - playing from the heart as it were."*

LOVE WITH WISDOM

Seeing the world through the eyes of the Loving Self can seem mystical at times. Space and even time seem to dissolve. In this mystical place, one can see beyond the physical appearance of someone, see beyond that momentary state of condition of someone, to see deep within them. In these moments, you can see the potential of that person's heart. You can see that we are all the same. It is impossible to hate when you can see these depths in another person.

Your Loving Self forms a bond of friendship with all the other Selves, a cooperative spirit, a harmonious cooperation. In this energy, you cannot help but express your Love with wisdom. You have resurrected your Heart and released the negative weight you have been carrying. It will become second nature to share your love, abilities, and wisdom with all those that are attracted to you. The rest of the world is free, without judgment, to grow or stagnate, to live or to die, to find their heart or continue to carry their negative weight.

Love and wisdom combine to empower your life. Life changes. Values and tastes change. Friends change. Relationships are healed or ended. Transition is a part of your life because of the many changes. Things are not like they used to be.

CREATIVE EXPRESSOR

"Believe in yourself! Have faith in your abilities! Without a humble but reasonable confidence in your own powers you cannot be successful or happy…formulate and stamp indelibly on your mind a mental picture of yourself as succeeding. Hold this picture tenaciously. Never permit it to fade. Your mind will seek to develop the picture . . . Do not build up obstacles in your imagination. Do not be awestruck by other people and try to copy them. Nobody can be you as effectively as YOU can."

~Norman Vincent Peale,
American minister and author, 1898-1993

Located at the throat, your Creative Expressor is first among the three highest Selves. It encompasses all our thoughts and feelings relating to expressing our abilities in the world, whether those abilities are expressed through the spoken word, writings, art, or other ways. Mature adults jokingly ask, "What am I going to be when I grow up?" When this Self is cleared of self-doubts and fears, the thoughts, feelings, and abilities of our true Expressor unite with our other Selves to be full expression of our qualities, talents, and contributions to life.

Sadly, many people have intentionally closed-off their Expressor, allowing strong fears and doubts to overtake their own expression. On the other end of that spectrum, there are also many people who misuse their expression – loudly and frequently. In these cases, people do not hold back, especially when they are expressing from anger. Venting one's anger and using one's expression as a weapon is not the true purpose of the Creative Expressor. It is possible for the unawaken Expressor to become a tool for the Emotional Self and Achiever to use or misuse as they will, for their own (and often hurtful) objectives.

Here is an interesting example.

John was a vice-president of a Fortune 500 corporation who found it very difficult to speak in business settings, especially in meetings attended by those who held high positions in their respective companies. Since his job required that he attend and speak at the board of director meetings of several corporations, his fear and discomfort in these settings were creating issues. John was known in these meetings as the silent member because he just could not make himself speak up when necessary. While he had no problem expressing himself in personal relationships or with the staff he managed, important business situations, like board of director meetings, left him tongue-tied, afraid that he would put his foot in his mouth.

*John came to me for help. During our sessions, as we began to dis-
cover the repressed thoughts and feelings of his Creative Expressor,
one image consistently emerged – the devil holding a pitchfork! As
we went further, John discovered that he saw his Creative Expressor
as an evil force, one that could injure others. He did not trust his
Creative Expressor, therefore, he would not express. He froze in
meetings because he did not trust his ability to express without being hurtful.*

*Where did this image and these thoughts originate? In John's case, it
was a past life. He remembered a situation where he was a Roman
orator and soldier. In this life, John was an eloquent, passionate,
even fiery, speaker, able to arouse and motivate crowds. He had
the ability to incite riots with his words. Before leading a group of
soldiers into battle, John rallied them with a passionate speech that
emboldened them and stirred their anger for the enemy. The entire
group of soldiers were killed in battle. John was the only survivor.
Deeply remorseful, he exiled himself and spent the remainder of his
life in silence, vowing never again to use his words to hurt another.*

*John realized immediate changes. He now understood why he did
not trust his ability to express. At the next board meeting, he gave
an eloquent presentation on the marketing of a new product –
and his audience, this group of directors, applauded. With his new
awareness, my client had freed his Creative Expressor. He knew
that he would never again misuse his ability to express.*

The Creative Expressor is a key part of our wholeness, yet it lies almost
dormant until the Loving Self is resurrected and free to love. These two
Selves serve as the directors of all the other aspects of Self. Imagine your
Sexual Self, taking its direction from this team, knowing just the right
heartfelt words to touch the heart of your partner, feeling, and expressing your true, loving nature. Wow! Talk about sex on Saturday night!

If you have never met your Loving Self or Creative Expressor, you are missing the fullness, a richness, in your life. If you doubt or distrust your ability to express yourself – or if you use your expression to control or manipulate others, you have not met your Loving Self or Creative Expressor.

The teamwork of the Loving Self and Creative Expressor is key to a happy Sexual Self. We must find our own loving expression. It does not matter what we have been taught in the past. We can choose how we use our ability to express. We can begin one step at a time. We can make it through one whole day with loving expression even if we had to say no to someone. We can feel good about ourselves at the end of the day. We can do it again the next day and the next.

LOVE EXPRESSED

When your Expressor works closely with the Loving Self, the tone of your voice begins to change. It becomes melodious and harmonious. The words travel to whomever you are speaking and gently touch them. The tone invites their participation either through listening or responding. I call this *magnetic expression*.

The tone of love has a charisma all its own. It is not the emotional fervor of an over-zealous preacher. It is not the 'twang' of an emotionally upset person. It is not the skilled tone of a professional speaker who pushes the ideas and information at you relentlessly throughout the presentation. It is not the tone of an entertainer who is performing to please or succeed.

The tone of love is a sharing experience. The recipient feels the words and internalizes them. The exchange is reciprocal. After the exchange, the truth of the speaker belongs to the recipient. When your Presence encourages your Loving Self and your Creative Expressor to represent your total being, you begin to share the things you love. The Loving Self is discerning. It only wants to share with those who have a desire to hear. The rest of the world is free to learn or listen to someone else. The Law of Attraction is the Law of Love. The tone of love always attracts love. A sensitive person can tell a lot from the tone of someone's voice. We can have facades, phony smiles, and deceptive words but the tone of our voice never lies.

THE INTUITIVE SELF, THE VISIONARY

The Intuitive Self, also called the Visionary, is the first of the two highest, mystical Selves. As such, we move into an area of function and purpose that includes intuition and connection to Source/God. The Intuitive Self is the source of all our perceptions, both conscious and unconscious. It is located right in the middle of our forehead.

The Intuitive Self lives is a timeless and spaceless zone. It is not limited by the boundaries of our three-dimensional, physical world. Every genius, every enlightened being who has ever walked in our world has known his or her Visionary. They have seen through their inner eyes to witness what *already was*, and channeled the concept, idea, invention, music, art, or technology into our world. They tapped the Universal Mind, also in our collective unconscious, and channeled what they saw, sensed, or heard into the world of form so it could benefit our world. Their inspiration is our gift. Were great individuals like Einstein or Tesla intuitive? Both were keenly aware that they were connected to something greater as the source of their inspiration.

The Intuitive Self provides our direction in both our outer, physical world and inner, intuitive world. When in cooperation with the rest of our Selves, we travel the Path with a sense of timelessness. Our movement is steady. Positive changes happen quickly. It is no longer surprising when something good happens. You know this is the way it always should have happened. Now you know why it is happening. The healthy Visionary continues to direct us to let go of old negative excess baggage, freeing us to embrace the new.

Most of us are familiar with the word "intuition." When the clouds of our negative emotions have been removed, we can hear the clear voice of our Intuitive Self. In this state of awareness, we intuitively understand the course of our lives, where we are going, and our sense of purpose. In this state of awareness, we may not have the details of how, what, when, or where because we trust that our lives are unfolding with purpose, we know we are attracting new experiences every moment. We are creating a new life through our ability to attract the positive and loving situations for ourselves. We begin to trust. We realize that we are trusting our Intuitive Self to guide us in the best direction, to say "no" when necessary.

Some people reading this will roll their eyes and think I am talking about becoming psychic. Oddly enough, the word psychic originated in Greece and means "pertaining to the human soul." It refers to human awareness and abilities that go beyond the five physical senses. In modern times, within our unaware societal constructs, it has become associated with charlatans or sideshow fun. Everyone is intuitive. Our Intuitive Self is our telepathic tie with all life. Everyone has an Intuitive Self. Everyone has a Visionary. Everyone can easily learn to trust their own intuition. The Intuitive Self is often ignored by those on the Expressway of Life. We rationalize our intuition away.

On the other hand, the unhealthy Intuitive Self can easily devolve into a harsh Judging Self. To awaken the full nature of the Intuitive Self, and keep that Judging Self from rising, it is necessary to remove the surface layers of negative self-judgment. As we clear away the negative thoughts and feeling, we discover a new sense of clarity; we begin to see things in our lives with objectivity, as they really are. It becomes much easier to evaluate our life experiences without emotion. With clarity, we can understand the lessons to be learned from our experiences and make wiser, more creative decisions about our future.

Without that discernment sharpened by clarity, we are destined to repeat our mistakes – and repeat them often. We already know that an unhealthy Emotional Self can continually create experiences filled with havoc, confusion, and leave us wondering what is wrong with us. How many failed relationships are necessary to choose a path of self-discovery and healing?

Lastly, the healthy Intuitive Self is the connection to one's memory of Source/God. The unaware Presence hears about information of this nature, labels it as God, and decides whether to believe or discard the information. Whatever your beliefs, through our Intuitive Self, you have access to all the information that is, was, or will be. We have the means to feel just how deeply we are connected to everyone and everything. Few of us, however, venture inward to discover the information, the truth. Even fewer experience the depth and brilliance of their true Intuitive Self.

THE ANGEL SELF

> *"The miracle is not to fly in the air, or to walk on the water, but to walk on the earth."*
>
> **~Chinese Proverb**

Our Angel Self, the seventh and highest frequency Self, is located at the top of the head. When we connect with our Angel Self, we begin to understand everything about our life – all the events, and the experiences, all the thoughts and feelings. Everything begins to have meaning, even the difficult experiences. It is easier to understand how each event carried us one step closer to becoming our highest Self, why we chose to step off the Expressway. It shines a light on one's growth as a connected and aware being. The aware Angel Self brings inspired thought, not just rational thought.

Our Angel Self continually whispers messages of encouragement and inspiration to the rest of our Selves. When we are traveling the Expressway of Life, we can rarely hear because there is so much noise. Our Angel Self, knowing that at some point in our journey we will eventually hear, forever persists in sending us messages. Our Angel Self knows the truth of who we are, sees our potential on Earth, and continually reaches out to help us become all that we are.

Our Angel Self understands and guides you toward your purpose. Without a sense of purpose, we can feel so insignificant and small in the grand scheme of life. With a sense of purpose, we become seed sowers of positive thoughts, pioneers of greater ways. You can realize your purpose at any time, even when doing what some would consider to be mundane things like washing dishes, taking a shower, or mowing the lawn. When that revelation happens, it is a divine event. The Angel Self has delivered its message right to the heart: I am unique and special, I matter, I have something to give to the world, I am important in the Divine Scheme of Things.

Our Angel Self knows that love and harmony are possible through the awakening of Self. It believes that love and peace is possible on the Earth – and that it begins within each of us. The Angel Self gives inspiration and encouragement to all our Selves. When the Loving Self, the Angel Self, and the Presence become one in purpose, love, and action, we walk our talk. We are at peace with ourselves.

Have you ever felt your Angel Self? When you have those persistent thoughts, however fleeting, that you have a purpose, a special reason for being on this Earth, you are feeling your Angel Self.

THE SUM OF OUR SEVEN MAJOR SELVES

In summary, each of our seven aspects of Self has a function, and each is an equally important part of who we are and how we function in the world. Each Self has its unique location in the physical body, starting at the sacrum at the base of the spine and progressively moving upward to the top of our head. And each of the seven Selves impacts the Sexual Self.

At each Self location, there is a nucleus. The energy from the Self radiates outward from this nucleus. That energy can be positive or negative depending on the awareness level of the Self. This means that each Self actively participate in one's emotional and physical health. Aware and healthy Selves radiate an aura of well-being and peace from their positive energy. The aware Self knows it is part of the Whole, never isolated or alone.

At their highest function, the healthy Selves do this:

- *The Angel One* **inspires our sense of purpose and kinship with all life,**
- *The Intuitive Self, the Visionary* **is our eye of perception and knows the history of our progress as an individual soul,**
- *The Creative Expressor* **lovingly expresses all our abilities through a variety of ways,**
- *The Loving Self* **empowers and directs our life with the primal force of love,**
- *The Achiever* **provides reason and accomplishment,**
- *The Emotional Self* **sustains our youth, vitality, sensuality, and enthusiasm, and**
- *The Presence* **represents all the other Selves to the world and owns our sense of self-esteem, confidence, and self-worth.**

The sum of all our Selves is who we are. We are not just our body or form. We are not just our emotions, or mind, or heart, or expression. We are an accumulation of all these things even if we are unaware of some of them. Know all the members of your team. Know all your potential and you will know Self. Only then will you have an inner team that works in cooperation for the greater good of you. Only then, will you have a healthy Sexual Self and sex on Saturday night!

> *Deep peace of the Running Wave to you*
> *Deep peace of the Flowing Air to you*
> *Deep peace of the Quiet Earth to you*
> *Deep peace of the Shining Stars to you*
> *Deep peace of the Gentle Nights to you*
> *Deep peace of the Son of Peace to you*
> *Moon and Stars pour their healing light on you.*
> *Deep peace to you.*

~A Gaelic Blessing

Chapter Three:

THE ARCHETYPES, OUR TEACHERS

WE HAVE LEARNED that we have a Sexual Self. We have learned that we each possess both male and female energies, the vibration of our Oneness. And, we have learned about our seven major Selves and their role in our lives. It is equally important to understand the forces outside of ourselves, especially the seduction forces, which can cause us to lose our way.

These forces are called archetypes. Archetypes are the accumulation of like energy in what we call the Collective Consciousness. Carl Jung used the concept of archetypes, a series of universal prototypes, in his practice. His grouping and naming of archetypes is the most recognized today.

So, archetypes are made of all the thoughts and feelings of each of us. Archetypal forces can also be our greatest teachers. Good, bad, or indifferent, each archetype exhibits unique characteristics and behaviors. Once understood, these characteristics and behaviors are easy to spot in others. It is more difficult and less enjoyable to recognize, much less acknowledge, the archetype behavior in ourselves. Sometimes we act out several archetypal behaviors at the same time. Certainly, at some point in our lives, we have exhibited most of the traditional archetypal characters over the course of our life.

When we do not have a strong sense of Self, we unknowingly borrow the power of archetypes to feel some measure of power. Essentially, we temporarily incorporate the power of an archetype within us (whether consciously or unconsciously) for a specific purpose or to supplement a part of us that we believe is missing. The need to assume the power of an archetype is usually triggered by an external situation that pokes at an internal repressed, faulty thought and our subconscious need to fill some perceived lack within ourselves. The power consumes us, becomes part of us, giving us a false sense of Self. It is possible to become stuck in an archetypal energy for an entire lifetime.

Much of our life we spend searching for approval. We seek approval first from our parents, then our peers, teachers, spouse, boss, and anyone who will recognize us. We all eventually evolve through our life experiences. Carl Jung calls this the natural process of individuation. He says that we spend the first half of our life with the underlying attitude of "What's in it for me?" The healthy person reverses this thinking in later life, embracing the thought, "How can I help others?" Remember this! It is essential to enjoying that intimacy that brings about sex on Saturday night.

To shift this thinking, we must develop some sense of goodness within our Self. The struggles we go through in the first half of our life sometimes leave such feelings of unworthiness and a sense of failure that we are not able to make the shift before we die.

At one time or another, we have felt seduced by forces in our world.

Anger has made us lose control, or strong sexual urges have gotten us into trouble. We have put people in their place, sometimes unnecessarily. These emotional bursts of intensity are common to us all. They happen fast and leave just as fast. We are not caught in them for more than a moment. We are not often obsessed by them, nor do we become them. Yet, there are times when we are consumed by negative thoughts and feelings to the point that they become our identity, creating dysfunction, and causing cycles of unhealthy behavior and life events. Understanding these outside forces enables us to acknowledge our behavior and look for a new way, a new means of living a life of fulfillment rather than struggle. It also enables us to understand the behavior of our life partners so we may engage in all interactions with awareness, patience, and love.

Is one archetype better than another? It is not a matter of better or worse. It is a matter of using a power other than one's own. It is also possible to move in and out of different archetypes at different times in one's life, searching for a sense of satisfaction and recognition. When we have high self-esteem, self-confidence, and self-worth, we have no need for their power. We feel our own power. We have our own unique sense of Self. We are free to envision and work towards the future of what we want.

Archetypal energy is always predictable. While each type exhibits its own characteristics, they all have predictable patterns. It is important to note that, while the following information is often expressed using masculine nouns and pronouns, both men and women can find themselves consumed in archetypal energy.

In this chapter, we will focus on the most prevalent and harmful archetypes, those archetypes that can create havoc in a relationship.

The Warrior

The Warrior archetype is the expression of anger. Anger is anger. The Warrior consists of all the anger in the world. Here is an example of being consumed by the Warrior.

George is standing alone at the party. No one notices him or acknowledges his presence. He feels isolated and lonely. Suddenly, George begins to feel angry. He wonders why no one notices him. He begins to think that no one cares, even his loved ones. Do they not see how special he is? The more these thoughts swirl in his head, the angrier he gets. The angrier he gets the more power he feels. Now he is attracting the angry energy of the collective consciousness and becomes the Warrior archetype. He becomes short-tempered, pompous, and rude to anyone who approaches him.

The Warrior's anger is a catalyst to give one a false sense of Self. The power comes on suddenly where none was felt before. When one is angry, things get done. People fear the Warrior. The Warrior has power. Warriors are always involved in conflict, confrontation, and war of one kind or another. When Warriors are without anger or a war, they feel nothing. There is no true sense of Self. So, to feel the power again, the Warrior must seek another just cause or battle to feel that sense of power.

In other words, every time we feel a strong sense of power when we are angry, we have attracted the Warrior archetype. The Warrior energy overpowers our sense of self that was weak and non-existent at the onset. Warriors enjoy physical, emotional, and mental confrontation of all kinds. The Warrior has a low boiling point, a quick temper, and an ocean of rage lying in wait just beneath the surface. This rage surfaces as constant irritation, prejudice, resentment, abuse, and any excuse to start a confrontation of some kind.

As with most archetypes, the Warrior has both positive and negative sides. Whether a gang leader or a police officer, anyone who has an affinity for violence and hatred is a Warrior. An abusive parent who physically violates their child, a spouse who abuses his partner, a person who is always battling issues for the righteous sake of justice, a boss warring with his employees, a mother warring at the PTA meetings, a criminal who takes what they want from others – these are all Warriors. Once we have incorporated the power of the Warrior, we become the Warrior. It is now our only sense of Self, our self-identity. Our life is one confrontation, battle, and war after another.

VICTIMS OF WARRIORS

When involved in archetypal energy, there is always an opposite side to the energy, like two sides of a coin. The Victim of the Warrior is the flip side of Warrior energy. At some point in time, our power gets too abusive for even us to handle and we are appalled at our own behavior. We vow never again to hurt others. We withdraw from the Warrior archetype, but never having developed our own sense of Self or self-identity, we feel nothing. There is nothing worse than feeling nothing.

We bury our last acts of abuse and confrontation deep in our heart so no one can see our dastardly deeds, not even ourselves. We vow never to hurt, abuse, or misuse our power again. Where does that leave us? It leaves us powerless. Since we cannot stand the feeling of nothingness or powerlessness, we vicariously begin to attract the power of the Warrior in a new way. We become Victims of the Warrior. We begin to attract situations and people that wage war on us.

We attract the Warrior situations and people because of its power. When we first become involved, we may not be consciously aware that we have attracted abusive Warriors. We are attracted to their presence and physical strength. We may feel safe because of his or her power.

Those individuals who have assumed the power of the Victim archetype are not aggressive and warlike. They are the victims who vicariously feed off the power of negative, chaotic, and violent people, events, and circumstances. They are Warriors, still energetically connected to that archetype, but functioning as its counterpart, the Victim.

Victim Warriors usually have deep feelings of unworthiness and feel undeserving of anything good, whether consciously or subconsciously. Many times, an abused wife stays with her abusive husband because of her undying love. Unfortunately, it is not this unwavering love that she is experiencing but an attachment to the power of violence and the Warrior energy. She has subconsciously chosen not to abuse her physical power but is tied to the experience of abuse through a psychic connection. Many times, individuals with this type of psychic connection, become involved in one abusive relationship after another or have one abusive boss after another. Some take this repeated cycle as a sign of suffering and often blame God for abandoning them.

The Warrior and Victim are strange bedfellows. The abuser and the victim need and energize each other. One does not have power or identity without the other. A husband cannot abuse his wife unless she is there and available to be abused. When a person becomes fed up with being abused or begins to develop a sense of self-worth, he or she walks away from the Warrior and the abuse. He or she begins to desire something greater than battle. The one who stepped away from the Warrior can create new, more positive experiences, and build a strong sense of Self. Often, when one Victim walks away, the Warrior will attract another Victim. The hellish cycle continues while the Victim who stepped away is never missed.

We can never find our real identity when consumed by archetypal energy. But as with all archetypes, we can learn and grow from the Warrior archetype. When we step back and look at our Warrior energy objectively, we can see it for what it is or was – a stage of learning that is not necessary to repeat. Anger begets anger. War begets more war. When we can begin to feel our own loving power, we no longer have a need to borrow the power of the Warrior or the Victim to feel a sense of Self.

Warriors and Victims provide the dark shadows in our world. They continue to perpetuate the hurt, violence, pain, confrontation, and war. We continually read about violence in the newspapers or hear about in news reports. It touches us in our homes, workplace, neighborhoods, and cities, sometimes in obvious ways, sometimes in subtle ways.

- *The wife who enjoys making love after a big fight.*
- *The husband who gets drunk and beats his wife.*
- *The mother who takes her frustration and anger out by verbally abusing her children.*
- *The father who punches walls and beats his son.*
- *The war mongers who create wars so they can engage.*
- *The prejudicial tyrants who belittle and cause pain to those who are weaker or different.*
- *The employee who is always stirring up trouble and keeping tempers boiling at work.*
- *The child who is a bully and the child who is being bullied.*

When engaged in a battle, Warriors and Victims feel power and vital energy. They are living in the illusion that they are feeling the power of Self. There is no true individuality for those caught in the archetypal energy of the Warrior. Warriors are clones of the collective anger and hatred of humankind. These energies are found in the Collective Consciousness, the accumulated thoughts and feeling of all humanity. When we become angry and resentful or want to aggressively right an imagined or actual wrong, we attract the Warrior energy and are consumed by it. Our anger increases ten-fold as we experience the power of the Warrior. We feel this borrowed power as self. When we are warring, we feel alive. We get hooked and feed from this archetypal energy much like leech feed on a host. If we get full and fall away from our host, the Warrior, we feel insignificant. We feel nothing. We seek to find another host to feed our false sense of Self. We seek another argument, fight, cause, or battle to feed our sense of importance and to feel life of any kind. We are completely immersed in Warrior energy. We are addicted to rage, battle, being right and a fight of any kind. Even when we are so saturated that we begin to back away, we have created a cord to easily find our way back to our host, the Warrior, and the battle.

In man's early beginnings, all men were warriors in a sense. Survival was the focus of each day. Tribes battled other tribes for dominance and survival. Fast forwarding to the twenty-first century, we find that, while man has evolved, the Warrior energy is still strong. On a global level, we see that energy in wars, authoritarianism, and discrimination. On the individual level, many of us have evolved beyond the Warrior despite the occasional relapse. Humanity, since its evolution from living in caves, desires something greater than confrontation.

THE WILDMAN

Those who have moved beyond the Warrior energy, but still do not have a good understanding of Self, often find that they still desire something – something that will make them feel good. Still unaware of the wisdom and knowledge within their Inner Space, they begin to search for pleasure outside themselves and discover the next archetype, the Wildman. Most of us have been the Wildman at least one time in our lives. Some of us are "stealth wildmen," unable to act upon their wild desires, but nonetheless, Wildmen in our thoughts and fantasies. Others have been stuck in Wildman energy for most of their lives.

Our desire for pleasure, to be saturated with pleasure, attracts the collective group energy of the Wildman. To the unfulfilled Self, the Wildman energy feels wonderful. When we are saturated and must stop to catch our breath, we feel empty. We feel a sense of nothingness. We must go out and fill ourselves again to feel good. ***The Wildman is a highly addictive archetype.*** It does not matter what the addiction, the Wildman must feel pleasure, vitality, to feel anything at all. But the feeling of pleasure always leaves, and the Wildman is caught in the addictive pattern of having to refuel. The foodaholic, chocaholic, sex addict, shopaholic, drug addict or alcoholic all have one commonality. Each addiction is the Wildman, perpetuating the energy of destructive desire.

Like the Warrior, the Wildman sustains the hurt and pain just in a different way. Unlike the Warrior, the Wildman does not like battle. The Wildman is only interested in saturating themselves with pleasure. Wildmen intensely dislike being controlled even though they are quite good at controlling others through their negative habits.

The Wildman is very prevalent in our world. It might be:

- The "ladies' man" who has many different sexual partners — different faces, different places.
- The woman who uses whoever is convenient to fill her insatiable sexual appetite.
- The person who "maxes out" his credit cards, yet still must buy things.
- That friend who goes to the bar every night and gets wasted.
- The thief who robs or steals to buy more drugs.
- The introverted family member who cannot stop eating.

The Wildman is continually looking for anything to make himself feel something, constantly trying to fill his unfillable Self. But the

Wildman's emotional needs cannot be fulfilled. The emptiness and pain always return and, again, the Wildman must scurry, deceive, connive, lie, over-indulge – anything to fill the emptiness and regain a feeling of power. One can never find true Self while stuck in the Wildman. This archetype is a massive energy of desire without wisdom, perpetuated by the greed, lust, and abuse in collective consciousness. The Wildman cannot be satisfied, and many people have died trying.

Overdose, obesity, alienation, and bankruptcy of body, mind and spirit is usually the result unless a new thought is birthed. Thoughts such as, "How can I help myself?" and "There must be something more to life than this." The new thought or question births the beginning of a new life, new learning, and eventually a new sense of the true Self, that Self imprisoned by the Wildman and now set free to find its unique individuality.

The Wildman, male or female, only sees others as a means to fill his needs. Often, relationships have regressed to being a mere duty or obligation. The Wildman is repulsed by duty. He glamorizes his image and lifestyle by thinking of himself as the wild child, the non-conformist, or the rebel when, in reality, he is a user, a taker, and a sensation addict who sustains the energy of greed, lust, and abuse.

Warriors and Wildmen are not bad individuals. In fact, they are not expressing any individuality at all. They are acting out archetypal energies. They have either lost touch with their Self or have never had a sense of Self. Both anger and rebellion can smother our true Self. We all have a rebel within us. When we lose touch with our innate wisdom and allow our rebel to wreak havoc on our life and our loved ones, we are lost in an archetype. Every angry person and every sensation addict can find reason to justify their actions. It is easy. They can blame the world, God, humanity, mother, father, sister, brother, ex-spouse, or spouse. People traveling on the Expressway of life constantly blame others. They do not have time for anything else. It is their sanity saver for things gone wrong.

Blaming others perpetuates victim energy. On the Path, one learns to stop placing blame. Taking responsibility for what happens brings the freedom to correct situations and bad relationships. New choices emerge, making it possible to exercise creative solutions. It takes time to be still and ask, "Why am I rebelling?" It takes faith in your greater Self to know you will hear the answer. It takes courage to hear the answer. Finally, it takes inner strength to act on the answer.

THE TYRANT KING

Dominating, domineering, and controlling tyrants are characteristics of the archetype known as the Tyrant King. Regardless of its name, this archetype energy can affect both men and women. While the following explanation of the Tyrant King uses male pronouns and references, both men and women are influenced by this archetypal energy. The Tyrant King must be right, must have the last word. To the Tyrant King, power and control are essential to success.

Aggressive, the Tyrant King intimidates his families, fellow workers, and friends. Money and power through fear or threat buy loyalty, friends, and favors. The Tyrant King must be on top or risk feeling helpless, so he will ruthlessly do whatever necessary to remain at the top. The person who is immersed in this energy is merciless and mercenary, oblivious to the value of others except in their value as servants to him. Others exist simply to serve him. While a true king is a willing servant to his people, the Tyrant King is incapable of serving others. His consistent threats, cold eyes, and hard heart make the Tyrant King an isolated, cartoon-like character.

The husband, acting as a Tyrant King, calls all the shots, approves, or disapproves what his wife and children can and cannot do. On the other hand, he could completely ignore his commitment to his family as he dallies in affairs, absorbs himself in his job, or devotes all his attention to his hobbies and activities outside the home. The wife, acting as a Tyrant Queen, rules her surroundings with an iron hand – and all must obey. She is an expert at manipulating power plays because she must have the controlling power. She is demanding and relentless with her rules, punishments, and rewards. She rules through fear rather than love.

The Tyrant King father bullies the coaches and uses his power to ensure his son gets on the basketball and soccer team. The Tyrant Queen mother expects her offspring to be a direct reflection of herself. When the child fails, often the Tyrant Queen mother withdraws her approval and her so-called love to show the young one what it is like without her support. Power is the Tyrant King's fuel, and, like a psychic vampire, they extract the power of others, using abuse, judgment, and criticism.

The Tyrant King, whether man or woman, is the oppressor in our society. They are not necessarily sophisticated or polished in their cravings and need for control. They are often open and verbal about their desire for control. They are often self-revering, blatant, and obnoxious. The Tyrant King is so enthralled with his self-importance, he rarely receives from others. In fact, he does not know how to receive whether it be love, kindness, or other positive feelings. Nor does he want to receive because it makes him feel vulnerable.

No one can live up to the Tyrant King's expectations. The unfortunate child, spouse, or employee who tries to win the King's love and approval by proving themselves, always falls short and continually feels unloved and unappreciated. Tyrant Kings must always be in control, at any cost. They drive themselves hard, sustained by the high energy they feel when usurping power from others. While Tyrant Kings typically lack any kind of sensitivity, they can, on occasion, be moved by powerful emotion. We can liken this to a Mafia boss sobbing at his aunt's funeral just hours before he guns down his latest enemy.

What do we learn from being a domineering, controlling tyrant? Submersion in the Tyrant King energy may feel satisfying at first, but eventually its negative aftermath leads one to realize that there must be a better way of being. We begin to realize that the Tyrant's need for control was really masking an overwhelming sense of helplessness. Eventually, every Tyrant King loses his power over others. But they do not go down without a tremendous struggle and fight to maintain power. When loss of that power is finally acknowledged, one has an opportunity to understand those feelings of helplessness and, with a new sense of humility, explore new avenues of living.

We learn from the Tyrant King that people are not our pawns. People are not there to serve us. When we reach this realization, we can transform that strength into true leadership. A true leader serves others. Our strength and abilities are to serve others. We learn to give up the power of force and adopt the power of love. Here is Sebastian's story:

Sebastian was a business tycoon. He owned a stock brokerage firm and had an impressive portfolio. He was a workaholic and deeply consumed by the energy of the Tyrant King. One day, Betty, his wife of twenty-one years, came to him and said, "Honey, now that the kids are gone, I would love to pursue a career in nursing. I have always wanted to be a nurse." Sebastian slammed his fist on the table and yelled, "No wife of mine will ever work. You have everything you need. You do not have to work. Forget it."

After recovering from the outburst, Betty sidelined her desire, but the yearnings grew even stronger. Again, she tried and, again, Sebastian raged about her place as his wife. He was completely insensitive to her needs as an individual. Several more times Betty tried different approaches with her husband – maybe not nursing, maybe just a job. Each attempt resulted in the same response which was basically "You do not need to work. We have plenty of money. Appreciate what you have."

Betty was really asking to find her own sense of identity. She wanted to feel a sense of Self, to experience life outside Sebastian's shadow. Sebastian saw his wife as being there to serve his needs. He never recognized her love and beauty as an individual.

One day at the office, Sebastian had a heart attack. All attempts to revive him failed and he was pronounced dead. Betty was devastated. She knew nothing about his business, nothing about his portfolio, nothing about their many stocks. She never made the financial decisions. Sebastian ruled his empire alone. Friends tried to cheer Betty up, but she was lost. She could not cope. Betty came to me about six months after her husband's death. Depressed, Betty was floundering through each day. She sought counseling and, with therapy, found her sense of identity and purpose.

We have all flirted with the Tyrant King archetype. It tempts us daily, tries to seduce us to wield our power over another. Whether the control is passive or aggressive, the Tyrant King is the antithesis of love. Love never controls.

The Lover

Everyone knows someone caught in the Lover archetype. Maybe it is you. When you are in love with love rather than the person, you are caught in the Collective Consciousness energy of the Lover archetype. Everyone loves a lover except the victim that has just been dumped. What is the difference in someone honestly in love and someone caught in the archetype? You know you are stuck in the archetype when you only feel power, vitality, and a sense of life when you are in love.

As with all archetypal energy, the Lover feels nothing within Self. The Lover only feels when in love with someone. This archetype teaches us about the heartaches and hardships of co-dependency.

The Lover is powerful and desires that feeling of euphoria that often comes at the beginning of a relationship. Unfortunately, the Lover cannot sustain a relationship. When the relationship ends, the Lover always feels empty because there is no sense of love within Self. The Lover must have someone to feel love. This archetype is best understood by example:

> *Jill is thirty-eight years old, married for ten years, and has two children. Her husband, Bob, is an account executive for a well-known corporation. Their marriage is routine, uneventful, no surprises, little interaction. The passion between the two has long subsided.*
>
> *Bored, Jill decided to return to her old job with a computer company. One day, she brushed against a good-looking man while getting a cup of coffee. She felt a certain electricity. Their eyes met for only an instant, but she felt something she had not felt in a long time. The next day, by coincidence, they again ended up at the coffee maker at the same time. They exchanged names and some chit-chat. All that afternoon Jill could not get her mind off Derek. After a few weeks of innocent flirting Derek asked Jill if she wanted to go to lunch. Jill knew that he was married but rationalized that anything that felt so good could not be wrong, so she agreed to go.*
>
> *One lunch led to another until they eventually arranged to meet that night for a drink. Jill went home that evening and asked Bob if he would mind looking after the children while she went shopping with a friend. Bob was happy to help and was happy Jill was*

doing something she enjoyed.

Jill felt nervous as she left the house. Twangs of guilt nudged her, but she pushed them away. After all, what was wrong with having a drink with a friend from work? Derek met her at a small bar across town. They had a few drinks and, before they realized it, hours had passed. Jill was hooked. She did not want to leave but she knew she must.

Like Jill, Derek's marriage was also without passion. In two short hours, they found many things in common. The next day at work, Jill found a note on her desk. She opened it and a warm feeling spread throughout her body as she read.

Dear Jill, I really enjoyed last night. I have not felt like that in years. Maybe we can do it again some time. Affectionately, Derek.

Jill did not work much that day. She could not keep her mind off Derek. She left the office early hoping to get her mind straightened out. But, at home, it was the usual uneventful routines —activities with the children, dinner, watching Bob in his favorite chair with his tablet, children playing video games before bedtime. Jill felt all alone. This was no different than most evenings. Why did she feel so alone tonight? She thought of Derek. Immediately feeling guilty, she tried to talk to Bob, but he was intensely focused one reading his social media posts. She withdrew to her bedroom. What had gone wrong with their marriage? Why wasn't it fun anymore? Where was the feeling?

Later that evening Bob wanted to have sex. He put her hand on his erection and said, "How about it?" Jill turned over and said, "Not tonight." She turned her back to him as she thought how crude he is. She felt more alive just talking with Derek. Eventually, she fell asleep.

Weeks passed. After several brief visits in the breakroom, they arranged to meet for lunch, but his time, at a quiet place out of town. Their hands touched and their hearts raced. They gazed into each other's eyes. They barely touched their food. They agreed to meet the following night for another drink. It was easier for her to leave this time. She was angry at Bob for being so unromantic and insensitive. In fact, she was beginning to feel he was boring. They did not have anything in common except ten years of marriage and two children.

Tonight, was the night. Derek was so romantic, full of compliments. They danced to her favorite song. Their bodies met as they looked deeply into each other's eyes. Their energies merged and they fully incorporated the energy of the Lover. They were both totally and completely in love with being in love. Before leaving, they planned another opportunity to spend an afternoon together. The feelings of love were becoming physical. The passion they felt for each other dictated their next meeting. Neither of them was seeking sex. The feelings of being in love were creating the natural passion of the Lover.

Jill became involved in a full-fledged affair. Her relationship with Bob grew colder and more estranged. Bob was not aware or sensitive enough to know what was going on. He withdrew further because of his confused feelings. He did not understand what was wrong. Jill was always complaining. Nothing he did was ever good enough anymore.

Several months later, Jill and Derek were sitting at their favorite bar when Jill innocently said, "I'll be so happy when we are together all the time." Without a hesitation, Derek said, "That can never happen, I would never leave my children." The mood instantly altered. Jill froze. Derek had repeatedly told her he loved her. She felt his love. Why was he saying this? He went on to explain that he had responsibilities and was not free to do what he wanted. Jill felt betrayed. She left angry and sad all at the same time. She ran out of the bar, crying all the way home. It was over. Her life was over. Love was not real. Her heart was broken. She felt like her love had been abused, like she had given her heart away only to have it crushed. She fell asleep that night feeling empty and alone.

From that night forward, she ignored Derek at work. The affair was over. Jill had been the victim of the Lover archetype energy. Derek had been in the Lover archetype for some time. Jill had been his fourth affair in eight years. Fortunately, Jill was able to return to her marriage, seek counseling and restore the spark in her marriage.

In Jill's case, she was ripe for the Lover's picking and became a victim to the Lover archetype. Derek, immersed in the Lover archetypal energy for a long time, lured Jill into that energy. In that energy, both Jill and Derek succumbed to the temporary feeling of "being in love." Jill was able to learn from the experience and mend her marriage. No doubt, Derek went on to find the next victim.

The Lover is sophisticated and always attracts individuals who are "ready for an affair." Those individuals are usually lonely, not feeling any affection and attention in their life. Affairs are easy. Both parties involved are giving their peak performance during the relatively short time they are together. No one can sustain peak performance for any length of time, much less all the time. Following the predictable pattern exhibited by all archetypes, when the affair ends (and it always ends), one leaves feeling empty and unfulfilled. To relieve the emptiness, many seek another affair which will end the same way; and, thus, the cycle continues.

The feelings of "being in love" are powerfully addictive. The Lover archetype presents the illusion of oneness with another. In that energy, we feel that we have found love through the fairy-tale partner, that perfect partner who will make us whole, the "true love" we read about in romantic novels. These feelings excite the unhealthy Sexual Self, but these feelings cannot be sustained without having a deep committed love. Craving those feelings and unable to learn from earlier experience, many of the Lover's victims go on to become sophisticated Lovers themselves, introducing other naive victims to the Lover archetype energy. On the other hand, some individuals avoid getting stuck in the unhealthy cycle of the Lover. These individuals have found the courage to step back from the experience and seek to know themselves in a new way. They discover that, with a healthy Sexual Self, they can love and be loved in a relationship that is deeply rooted in the Heart.

Lasting true love, like affairs, is also a feeling of oneness. However, lasting true love goes much deeper than the ego-oriented Lover energy. True love is characterized by compassion, understanding, wisdom, and a desire for harmony. Only a healthy Self, including the Sexual Self, can sustain a lasting true love. Caring, as well as a value for harmony, silences the urge to yell at your mate when in a bad mood. With love and wisdom, one intuitively knows the appropriate time to speak about important matters. Love and understanding forgives mistakes and errors in judgment. Love and compassion are sensitive and lend a healing word or hand when needed. Love is being thoughtful in practical ways every day.

To genuinely love another, one must first love one's Self. Life pulls on us in many directions — work, children, responsibilities – all of which usurps one's energies, leaving little time for one's own nurturing and well-being. The greatest joy of knowing Self is knowing one's Loving Self, knowing both one's imperfections and progress toward a healthy Self, including a healthy Sexual Self.

The Great Deceiver, the Trickster

The Great Deceiver, also called the Trickster, is the most powerful and dangerous of all the archetypes. Why? The Great Deceiver can work in conjunction with all other archetypes. When in the Trickster energy, an individual can quickly deceive whoever he wants, whenever he wants. He is the mighty controller.

In Trickster energy, one is compelled to take what one wants and step on anyone necessary to get what one wants. Lie, cheat, steal – the most cunning gets the prize. Be horrible and despicable today; tomorrow you can be good. The Trickster argues that goodness vanishes with a breath, goodness never lasts. The Trickster constantly points out one's flaws, shortcomings, and hurtful actions. One begins to feel bound to the Trickster and unable to break free because one begins to believe that he or she IS evil. The only power is the Trickster's power. The individual becomes nothing, a pathetic person to be trampled by the world. Self-destruction, self-deception, and self-hatred are the ultimate outcomes of being stuck in the Trickster archetypal energy.

Always the great manipulator, the Trickster can seduce through religion, science, politics, and industry. For example, many religions use fear to capture and hold its followers with statements like, "Believe in Jesus Christ as your savior or you will go to Hell." He uses our past mistakes and self-judgments to create an even deeper sense of unworthiness. How can such an unworthy soul get to heaven? In this scenario, one wants to find someone who will save them from the terrible fate of living for Eternity in Hell.

If the devil were an entity outside of one's own ignorance of thought, he would be the Trickster. As with all archetypes, the Trickster is derived from the Collective Consciousness, spanning from our early ancestors to the deceptions of today. With its many faces and shapes, the Trickster uses our own deep thoughts and desires about Self to manipulate, seduce, and deceive. This is an important aspect of how the Trickster works – it is our own thoughts of greed and desire to be the best rather than thoughts of always doing our best that attracts the power of this archetype. The Trickster feeds on others for self-gain, plays with others as a cat toying with a mouse. The Trickster is an expert at subliminal subterfuge, implanting thoughts of our eternal damnation and worthlessness. He does this with gusto. Those immersed in Trickster energy are limited in their ability to grow spiritually or maintain good health.

While the Tyrant King dominates through mental power (left brain), the Trickster moves beyond the limits of the left brain and taps into one's undeveloped psychic power to serve itself. The Trickster is the only God, according to the Trickster. There is nothing permanently good. All people can be deceived and will deceive through their greed. We see proof of this in our world daily. Our own lack of self-knowledge binds us and allows us to buy into the concept. Guilt, error in judgment, and our own insecure thoughts nurture the Trickster.

Adolph Hitler was a prime example of someone consumed by the Trickster archetype energy. Utilizing his charismatic magnetism and the power of his speechmaking, he seduced a nation into believing their own supremacy over all others. Self-power was Hitler's motivation, not brotherly love.

The Trickster will even try to dissuade the decision to exit the Expressway with comments like "You're wasting your time" or "You're going off the deep end." When we allow our thoughts to expand and venture away from collective consciousness, the Trickster's energy will be quick to tell us that there is nothing more to life than the Expressway. The Trickster tells us, "This is it. There is nothing better for you." Even though we feel better and like exploring the Path, the Trickster will take advantage of any remnant of doubt to foster more doubt. When someone tells us how wonderful we are, we think to ourselves, "Boy, are they dumb! If they only knew the real me!" It is too easy for the Trickster archetype to prey on old negative thoughts and on our fears of the unknown.

Knowledge is golden. When we understand the archetypal forces, especially the Trickster, we can recognize and understand their power and choose to use our loving power.

THE SAVIOR

The Savior archetype has strong seductive powers. It seduces us through our need to be needed. The Savior only feels worthy when rescuing and feels powerless and unworthy when there is no one to rescue. So, the Savior is perpetually trying to rescue people who *he* believes require rescuing. In the Savior archetypal energy, one believes that he is here to save the world. But the world does not want to be saved. The world is perfectly happy evolving as it is.

The victim of the Savior archetype is, ironically, the person being saved. By his very nature, the person targeted to be saved cannot be saved, otherwise he would not need saving. Only when an individual decides he wants to change will that individual seek solutions and take action to change his life.

Saviors live with the frustration of attempting to save people who cannot be saved. They have a knack for finding the strays, whether those strays are people or animals. Does it mean that anytime someone helps another that one is consumed in the Savior archetype? No! One is only consumed in Savior energy when one only attempts to rescue people who have not asked for help.

Imagine going to a homeless shelter carrying a suit, shirt, and tie. Then, singling out a homeless man you think needs help, giving the man the suit, and announcing that the suit will help the man get back on his feet. Imagine following that with an offer to house and feed the man in your home for a month while he looks for a job. You are met with incredulous skepticism. If the homeless man had wanted the responsibilities that go with a suit and job, he would have sought those things himself. In this scenario, the Savior energy wanted to save someone who did not desire to be saved. The Savior energy brought about a feeling of power.

Archetypal energy is always there, always ready to consume those who seek power and a sense of worth outside themselves. Knowing these negative influences is vital to knowing yourself. We interact daily with individuals who are functioning as the Warrior, Wildman, Tyrant King, or other archetypes. As one grows in one's understanding of Self, one finds the ability and courage to resist the temptation to attack another, use others, dominate, and reduce others to less than one's self. Instead, one's true Self, the loving Self, guides one's choices and actions. It is from a healthy Sexual Self that one finds that meaningful, from-the-Heart, relationship.

You will still make mistakes because you are a spiritual being learning to be a human being. You will be able to forgive yourself because you are aware of your mistakes. Forgiving and loving Self are the key components of a new alternative lifestyle. The path allows you to be gentle with Self and others. Understanding replaces blame. Wisdom replaces judgment. Harmony replaces chaos. Love replaces isolation and resentment.

Chapter Four:

HOW TO GET THE THRILL BACK

BY NOW, THIS is no real secret. The best way to "get the thrill back" is to detach from any archetypes and heal your Selves. Living from one's true Self, balances and heals the Sexual Self – and results in sex on Saturday night.

Interestingly, the Earth and its upkeep pose a great analogy. Just like we can pollute the Earth, we can pollute our energy with negative thoughts and beliefs. Just as we can clean up pollution and take measures to maintain a clean Earth, we have the tools and ability to "heal" our Self of thoughts and beliefs that not only limit our understanding of our true Self but that also keep us in shadow and dysfunction. The journey of self-discovery, of knowing Self, is fascinating, challenging, a little frightening. But, to do so reveals the beautiful truth of Self and brings the most amazing awareness and insight. The discovery and release of old thoughts and beliefs that are limiting one's fulfillment in life has great therapeutic benefit and leaves one's creativity wide-open to new and amazing ideas. The discovery of new abilities adds a dimension of interest to every moment, sparking a desire and courage to blaze new trails and experience new adventures. False pride and arrogance fall away. Anxiety and daily pressure fall away.

Self-understanding allows you to address emotional issues that are both limiting and dysfunctional. The means to gain self-understanding are both doable and repeatable. With self-understanding, you release your past guilts and self-condemnation and propel yourself into self-discovery. You learn to recognize sabotaging behavior. You make conscious decisions about the source of your thoughts and feelings as well as whether those thoughts and feelings deserve your energy and attention. You will find it easy and natural to create rapport and interact with those of your choice. You will grow in self-esteem and self-worth. Your mistakes will become more sophisticated as you learn new lessons instead of repeating the same old mistakes. You will be at peace even when you make mistakes because you have the means to learn from them and move forward with creative solutions that bring even greater results.

Acknowledging your worth is essential. ***You are important!*** This acknowledgment is not about ego – it is about accepting the full and wonderful nature of who you are. Everyone in your life will benefit from your self-awareness and acceptance. Remember that having a secure sense of Self and self-understanding will enable and empower you to be more loving and tolerant towards yourself and others. This newly found interest in Self provides the nurturing your Self needs to be fully expressive in the world. You will notice that you have more time for you, more time for others, and more time to do the things you love.

Are you ready to pursue a lifestyle of self-discovery, mystery, curiosity, and adventure?

Your new awareness will manifest in your life as greater peace, self-esteem, creativity, success, and a sense of freedom to follow your visions and the loving feelings in your heart. You see the world with new eyes. The sense of freedom is priceless. The feelings of abundance are pure gold.

So, where to begin? How does one get a grasp on something so large as one's Self? Most people, when they think about Self, narrow it down to a good self and a bad self, thinking "One day I care about people and things. That is my good self. The next day I do not give a damn. That is my bad self." We are much more than that.

This chapter includes practical ways to understand your Self, including exercises and recommendations to help you on your new journey. It is time to forgive yourself and forgive others in your life so you can take the needed steps toward a healthy Sexual Self.

STEP 1: EXIT THE EXPRESSWAY!

Make the conscious commitment to step off the Expressway and onto the Path.

Where does one begin to restore a healthy Sexual Self? It all begins by exiting the Expressway and taking the first step on the Path to the Heart, the path to self-discovery, wellness, and fulfillment.

We learned in Chapter 1 how most of us just exist on the Expressway of Life, speeding and careening down that expressway, too busy to enjoy life, too busy avoiding or ignoring our own shortcomings and those we love. This is understandable. To face your shortcomings is scary. It can feel like you are powerless – and feeling powerless is devastating. People wonder why alcoholics, addicts, or tyrants cannot just stop their abusive behavior and change instantly. While miracles can and do happen, changing addictive behavior is difficult. When they are not in the archetype, they feel nothing. The need to feel, the need for some sense of identity and power drives them into the repetitive patterns of their archetype. It is difficult to change. It is frightening to change. It takes courage to step away from a familiar, yet dysfunctional, lifestyle. It takes courage to say "no" to archetypal energy. Therefore, is it often a life-threatening trauma that jolts the desire for change. Healing begins with the desire to heal. Healing begins when one's desire to change becomes stronger than his or her fear of searching within themselves to discover the beautiful and vibrant nature of Self.

Moving from the Expressway to the Path to the Heart can feel, at times, like straddling two worlds. This temporary discomfort is well worth it. Anyone reading this book has already made the choice to change their life but are still experiencing stress, anxiety, and other overwhelming feelings. It is a difficult period, straddling the middle with one foot on the Expressway and one foot on the Path. The split that occurs from holding on to the old ways is painful. **One cannot hold on and let go at the same time.**

Choosing the Path is changing lifestyles even though, in the beginning, one continues to do many of the same things. Choosing the Path means quality, not quantity, peace, not speed, vitality, not fatigue, self-evaluation, not condemnation, and trust not fear. There is joy in the many moments of the day rather than waiting for the grandiose event that brings instant happiness. It is difficult to let go of old behavioral patterns and habits; it is unrealistic to think you can release all of them at one time. Behavioral change occurs as one becomes aware of the reasons for the behavior. As the change begins, positive feedback motivates the desire to continue to change.

The old habit of allowing no time for Self is the most difficult to release. Duties, family, and work try to demand 100% of one's time. It is necessary to let go of some of the unnecessary trivia and replace that trivia with things that are more valuable to one's peace and growth.

Selectivity becomes important on the Path. Remember, the Expressway allowed no time for Self. On the Path, there is time to be sensitive to one's own feelings, as well as the feelings of others. Quality not quantity time with Self is most important.

Once you step off the Expressway, it becomes much easier to see just how deeply archetypal energy has influenced your behavior. It then becomes easier to step out of that archetypal energy. We see through clearer eyes as we slowly begin to know and trust Self. We stop the self-sabotage and other emotional setbacks. Stepping off means embracing and enjoying your Loving Self as you heal and restore all aspects of Self, including the Sexual Self. It means forgiving Self and others for past hurts that occurred on the Expressway while engrossed in archetypal energy.

Over the years, many of my clients and students have made the choice to walk the Path. They have chosen a way of life that promotes self-discovery and personal growth. In the twenty-first century, world events are leading even more people to understand Self so they can be a positive force in that world. Today, more than ever before, individuals from all levels of society are searching for greater purpose and new directions in their life. They are searching to understand themselves. More people are conscious of taking care of their own health through nutritional wisdom. More people who experienced physical or sexual abuse, who have hidden their guilt and shame for years, are stepping forward seeking refuge and help. Others have become outspoken against prejudice and injustice. Many are helping others to heal.

Thousands of alternative and holistic health practitioners are teaching people how to take responsibility for their own health. Spirituality continues to move beyond the walls of religious dogma as more people look inward to explore the spirituality within Self, meditating and seeking to know the God within.

So, now is the time.

- *It is a time to muster all our strength and goodness to direct our lives on a positive, loving path.*
- *It is a time to take responsibility for our own actions and stop looking to others to see what we should do.*
- *It is a time to go within and discover Self, so we are less susceptible to archetypal energy.*
- *It is a time to choose positive, constructive, and loving thoughts by releasing negative thought and behavioral patterns.*
- *It is a time to forgive ourselves and others so we may step into the fullness of our qualities, strengths, and creative talents.*
- *It is a time to remove fear from our relationship with God by discovering that God-Spark within ourselves.*
- *It is a time of personal spiritual revolution.*

As a psychotherapist, I have encountered countless wounded and scarred individuals from dysfunctional families, families that have been stuck in one or more archetypal collective consciousness energies. Through my experimentation and exploration of the human psyche, I have developed repeatable processes to identify and release the pain, trauma and faulty thoughts that prevent us from expressing our own unique Self.

The field of human potential is fascinating. Unlike mathematics, taking away two weaknesses from a weak person result in a weaker person. On the other hand, adding one strength and taking away two weaknesses results in a stronger person. By feeling a sense of strength, individuals are more willing to let go of a weakness. On that premise, individuals can make incredible headway in their discovery of Self in a short time. Qualities and strengths are many times covered over and hidden from conscious awareness. Our qualities and strengths are within each one of us. They are inherent in our nature. It is more than possible to surface, recognize, and use those qualities and strengths.

> "People travel to wonder at the height of mountains, at the huge waves of the sea, at the long courses of rivers, at the vast compass of the ocean, at the circular motion of the stars; and they pass by themselves without wonder."
> ~ St. Augustine, theologian, and philosopher

Our personal growth on the Path would be incomplete without considering how we interact with others and why others behave the way they do. Understanding archetypes brings understanding of behavior in ourselves and others. Beyond recognizing the behavior, we do not have to understand a person's reason for being where they are. We do not even have to like it. We do have to allow them their freedom to evolve as they choose. We can then accept our own freedom to make our choices without guilt. We cannot control people or make them change because we want them to change. Each of us has free will and must exercise it in our own way. When most of us see someone hurting or living in a way that is harmful or dangerous, our heart wants to help, particularly when it is one of our loved ones. It is difficult to accept that they must learn from their own experience, that change will only occur when they choose to change.

Remember, the Expressway appears to be the fastest way. There is no time to probe the mysteries of Self. There is only time to skim the surfaces of what appears to us through our physical senses. We perpetually bring our ancestral thought, "I must struggle for everything I get", rather than realizing our nature as inspired creators. "Everything I touch turns to gold" and "Everyone I love becomes light" are the thoughts of a loving creator who manifests abundance in all forms. Abundance is the physical nature of God. Everything we touch becomes abundant. Everyone we love lifts into higher thought. Our higher thoughts are for the good of all.

STEP 2: DISCOVER YOUR INNER SPACE

We human beings have developed the technology to explore outer space. We can access information from around the world in seconds through computer technology and the internet. We have explored what makes up the atom through quantum physics. We have become environmentally aware, realizing that we must love and care for our planet. We have made new and astounding breakthroughs in many areas of science – all important but outwardly focused things. Yet, we give little attention to exploring inward, discovering all the aspects of ourselves and why we behave the way we do.

Our next great frontier is Inner Space, the discovery of Self. Years ago, I earned a degree in Behavioral Science only to discover that something was missing. The element of Heart was missing, that inward awareness that turns knowledge into wisdom had been completely overlooked. Over the years, I have devoted my efforts to helping others understand themselves. I started by experimenting, working with small groups. The more I did this the more I realized that knowing Self was a science, a process, that anyone could master.

When we seek to discover ourselves, we go inward to our Inner Space for information. Our Inner Space is our gateway to all the wisdom of the Universe – but it is also our own personal library, a library that contains all our thoughts and feelings. Each time we go to our Inner Space Library, we have access to our history, our "blueprint." Each shelf, each book exists in the deep recesses of the unconscious mind.

This personal library has seven stories, one floor in the library for each aspect of Self. The ground floor contains all the thoughts and feelings associated with our Presence. The second floor is filled with thoughts and feelings of the Emotional Self. As we go up, each floor corresponds to the seven major aspects of Self in order until we get to the seventh floor, the floor of the Angel.

Just like we browse through the books on the shelves of our community library, we will be browsing through the books in our personal library to understand the important aspects of Self and to discover why we behave the way we do. We walk through each floor to identify our thoughts and feelings, to reexamine our life experiences, to understand why we do the things we do.

Imagine yourself standing at the front door of your Inner Space library. Go in and look around. Take the elevator to explore other floors. As you become familiar with your Inner Space, you will realize that you can come to this library whenever you desire. Relaxed, with eyes closed, try visiting your Inner Space library with a specific intent or question in mind – for example, when did I begin believing that I must do everything myself? Enter the front door with the expectation that you will know where to go and what to do to receive your answer. Follow your intuition. It is quite amazing how this works.

Visit your Inner Space often. Understanding Self strengthens your sense of identity which, in turn, opens your life to all its grandest potential. Looking within means dissecting yourself – not the body, but rather, separating and singling out each major aspect of Self. Only in this way are you able to know your total potential and your needs. Then, you will know the many ways to enhance, empower and enrich your life.

STEP 3: KNOW YOUR CIRCLE OF INFLUENCE

To get a good grasp of Self, we must look at Self in relationship to the whole. Imagine standing, alone, with your thoughts and feelings. You are surrounded by a circle of people. These are the people that directly or indirectly influence your life. Their thoughts and feelings are constantly bombarding and effecting you. Beyond the people who are close to you, there is another circle of people. This outermost circle consists of everyone else in the world with all their thoughts and feelings indirectly or subliminally affecting you.

All the thoughts and feelings of everyone, including your own, make up the Collective Consciousness. In addition to your own thoughts and feelings, the negative and positive thoughts and feelings of this collective consciousness influence you daily. This is especially true if you do not have a strong secure sense of Self. When you know Self, you can choose to be inspired by the positive and constructive thoughts that rise and prevent the negative ones from entering your Inner Space.

> *"You are not your father. You are not your mother. You are not any of your relatives. You are not your teachers at school, nor are you the limitations of your early religious training. You are Yourself. You are special and unique, having your own set of talents and abilities. No one can do things exactly the way you can do them. There is no competition and no comparison. You are worthy of your own love and your own self-acceptance. You are a magnificent being. You are free. Acknowledge this as the new truth for yourself. And so it is."*
>
> **~ Louise Hay, motivational speaker, and author, from her book *Heart Thoughts***

When you imagine this scene, you can begin to see how easy it is to get caught up in the thoughts and feelings of others, all clamoring to influence you. You can begin to see how easily you could lose the sense of your own unique self and your own ability to think clearly and initiate creative solutions. Often this begins at home.

Most of the time, we grow up in a family where each member deals with emotional issues, faulty thoughts, and misbeliefs, moving in and out of various archetypes. We begin to deduce that this is just the way people are. Rarely do we say to ourselves, "I wonder if Dad knows that he is stuck in the Warrior archetype," or "Mom's issues with abandonment and helplessness are very apparent today." I have counseled so many individuals that grew up hating the prejudices of their parents and despising their intolerance only to adopt those behaviors in their own style as adults. Why does someone duplicate what he hates? Our parents, grandparents, and other relatives are far more influential than we realize. For years, they are our role models, good or bad. Day after day, we are influenced by their thoughts and feelings. Without conscious effort, their thoughts become our thoughts. We continue their prejudices and opinions without thinking for ourselves.

When we are struggling with our own identity, we subconsciously copy our role models. No one consciously decides, "I will become like my father, even though I hated that he never spent any time with me. Even though, I despised the way he dominated and traumatized my mother. Now I am going to act the same way with my wife and children." We cannot be that honest because we do not know ourselves well enough to be honest. It is much easier to blame others.

How were you influenced by your family and close friends? What ideas and misbeliefs did you acquire from them? Take a moment and ask yourself:

- How am I influenced by my father? What thoughts and beliefs did I acquire from him that are no longer serving me in a healthy way? How do I behave under this influence?
- How am I influenced by my mother? What thoughts and beliefs did I acquire from her that are no longer serving me in a healthy way? How do I behave under this influence?
- How am I influenced by my grandparents? What thoughts and beliefs did I acquire from them that are no longer serving me in a healthy way? How do I behave under this influence?
- How am I influenced by my closest friends? What unhealthy thoughts and beliefs are triggered when I am around them? How do I behave under this influence?

- How am I influenced by my boss and work colleagues? What unhealthy thoughts and beliefs are triggered when I am around them? How do I behave under this influence?
- How am I influenced by the news and social media? What unhealthy thoughts and beliefs are triggered by those sources How do I behave under this influence?
- How am I influenced by archetypical energy in the Collective Consciousness? What unhealthy thoughts and beliefs are triggered under this influence? How do I behave under this influence?

STEP 4: EVALUATE YOUR SELVES

Get to know all your Selves. The health of your Sexual Self is dependent upon the healing of your seven major Selves. Once you get to know your Selves, touch base with them on a regular basis. Check in to see how they are doing, to understand what issues or negative thoughts may have surfaced.

Your Inner Space library holds all the information you need to evaluate and understand each of your Selves. Here is an effective exercise of self-discovery, where we look inward, into our Inner Space, to discover our thoughts, feelings, and behaviors within each Self. This exercise is a guided visualization that provides an opportunity to observe each of your Selves, just as that Self is at the present time. There are specific things important to observe to better understand how this Self is impacting the Sexual Self.

The guided meditation below can be used with each Self. Start with the Presence and work up through all the seven major Selves as follows:

- The Presence
- The Emotional Self, also called the Inner Child
- The Achiever Self
- The Loving Self

- The Creative Expressor
- The Intuitive Self, also called the Visionary
- The Angel

In this exercise, we ask the Loving Self to help us as we evaluate each Self. Love is a powerful, primal force that, when set in motion, creates profound change. Through the Loving Self, we can begin to love all our Selves. You soon realize that it does not matter what you have done or what has been done to you. Understanding leads to forgiveness. Forgiveness leads to love. Love leads to healing. Healing leads to purpose, joy, and abundance.

Insensitive and unaware, many people only look at the surface of their issues. Now that you are off the Expressway of Life, you now have the time, desire, and commitment to go inward, to go deeply into the recesses of your Inner Space to discover, understand, and heal.

So, have your journal open and ready for notetaking!

EVALUATING THE SELF-GUIDED VISUALIZATION

1. Close your eyes and feel yourself relaxing. Take a couple of deep breaths, relaxing more with each exhale.
   a. Call to your [Self, i.e., Presence, Emotional One, etc]. Ask your [Self] to stand in front of you. You can see your [Self] clearly and in detail.
   b. Observe this Self exactly as s/he is. Start at the feet and slowly direct your gaze up until you see this Self's head.
   c. Observe without judgment. Notice how this Self is dressed, how s/he looks, what s/he is doing, how is s/he behaving.
   d. If this Self seems lifeless, call out to it again and ask it to return to your body. Watch for a change in this Self, then observe.
   e. On occasion, your [Self] might say something. This is OK, just write down what is said.

2. Record your observations, general feelings, and other information about this Self by filling in the blanks of these statements.
    a. I feel my [Self] is_____.
    b. I like these things about my [Self]: _____.
    c. I observed these positive things about my [Self]: _____.
    d. I observed these negative things about my [Self]: _____.
    e. The first thing I will do to help my [Self] is _____.
    f. Send our love over to this Self. Speak to it from a place of compassion. Forgive, if necessary. Ask to be forgiven, if necessary. Remind this Self that you need it to be a healthy part of the whole.
    g. You will intuitively know when the visualization is complete.
    h. Open your eyes. Write down the details of this visualization. Remember to do the things that you have written.

Each Self will have its unique appearance and will display its unique characteristics. While you might find similar observations among your Selves, there are more likely to be differences, differences related to the unique purpose of that Self. Here are some observation examples.

Seven Major Selves	Example of Observations
Presence	• My presence did not seem to be enjoying life, it was more a duty. • I saw a blank look, like my Presence was not "at home." • He was not focused, seemed to be far way.
Emotional Self	• I saw sadness in the eyes and a sense of helplessness. When I looked deeper, I saw confusion and anger. • I saw cold eyes. When I looked deeper, I saw anger and rage. • Felt like no one was a home. When I called my Emotional Self back into my body, I saw futility and loneliness. • I saw self-confidence and peace.
Achiever	• I saw fatigue. When I looked deeper, I felt a sense of being overwhelmed with life. • I saw cold, hard eyes. When I looked deeper, I saw disdain and judgment. • I saw darting eyes and scattered focus. • I saw confidence and compassion. • I saw a tyrant. When I looked closer, I saw fear.
Loving Self	• He smiled at me with such compassion. • She seems sad. • There was no life in his eyes.
Creative Expressor	• I saw eyes looking downward, afraid to make contact. • I saw lips tightly closed and deeply frowning. • Expressor is waving as if s/he is trying to get my attention. • I saw confidence and compassion.
Intuitive Self	• I saw a deep thinker. • I saw a person in judge's robes, shaking a finger at me. • Her eyes were closed, she was avoiding looking at me.
Angel Self	• He seems disheartened and tired. • She was glowing and smiling, happy to see me. • He seems distracted and unfocused.

Visit each Self on a regular basis. If you are experiencing something in your life that requires attention, use this visualization to understand and heal.

STEP 5: START EACH DAY IN A POSITIVE WAY

Begin your day by making a conscious effort to understand your emotional, physical, and spiritual state – mind, body, and spirit. Remind yourself that today you walk the Path, that today you choose to focus on higher things and to be mindful of the activities of your day. This just takes a little concentration and mindfulness.

Concentration is the ability to focus. Mindfulness is being present in each moment, fully in your body and aware of what you are doing and why. If you are in the energy of escape and avoidance, you may not be fully in your body. You must be in your body to have a healthy, loving, abundant, joyful life while you are on Earth.

Concentration and mindfulness minimize distraction and scattered thought. They are your compass while walking the Path. Mindfulness is the ability to remember what you are doing and where you are going. Mindfulness is also remembering that the Spirit within your heart is transforming your life. A focused mind and a state of mindfulness is your spiritual and emotional compass. It is the foundation of your resolve and discipline to stay on the Path of self-enlightenment. No doubt you have noticed that the Path is much narrower than the Expressway. Concentration and mindfulness diminish distraction and scattered thought. Like staying physically fit, concentration and mindfulness become stronger with conscious use.

Are your thoughts clouding your concentration and mindfulness? As you know, the Sexual Self is affected by the thoughts that spring from your Selves and the archetypal energy in the Collective Consciousness.

By now, you have come to understand and release any negative thoughts and feelings arising from these sources. Even though we may have a better understanding of our Selves, those negative thoughts and feelings can reappear at any moment, triggered by any number of things.

Now that you are aware of these thoughts and feelings, you may not only recognize them more quickly when they appear, but you may also make a choice to direct your energy elsewhere. Negative thoughts and feelings are fueled by emotion. You have a choice. You can refuse to fuel the negative thought or feeling. Or, instead of fueling those thoughts, allowing them to build up inside you until it explodes as reactive behavior, you can choose to let those thoughts and feelings go. Instead, fuel your positive thoughts and feelings. It is easier than you think.

STEP 6: DO A QUICK FEELING ASSESSMENT

Because we are energy – our thoughts, feelings, intentions, desires, even our physical bodies – we are constantly interacting with our energy and all the energy of those around us. We can easily absorb the energy of others from their thoughts and feelings. Or, as we noted above, a troublesome thought or feeling may be emerging from one of your Selves. There are times when a quick assessment of your feelings is helpful. Perhaps the in-laws are coming to visit, or you have an important conversation with your spouse coming up. Or you have a list of to-dos that just do not seem to get done. While it would be helpful, there are times when it may be impractical to do an evaluation of the Selves to flush out your feelings.

Instead, go a quick assessment of the three basic states of feeling. There are three distinct states of feeling – resistance, escape, and acceptance. Everyone, at any given moment, is typically in one of these three states, often moving among them. However, some people, especially the unaware, stay in one of these states most of the time. Interestingly, there is quick way of assessing your state of feeling – and, through observation, the state of feeling of others. Ask yourself the following three questions.

1. Am I feeling resistant? If so, why?

If you answered "yes," you are in a state of *resistance*. I call this energy the state of "resistance" because, in this energy, you attract to you people and situations that are the exact opposite of what you are moving towards. In other words, it feels like you are going backwards from your goals like the proverbial "taking two steps forward and one step back." In this energy, some aspects of Self resist when the physical body moves forward. The emotions do not want to go where the body is going. The mind is not interested in where the body is going. It is resisting what it thinks is its duty. The spirit can also resist if it is something that is unnecessary or will have a negative effect on the body.

It is the state of resistance that causes the most tension and stress on the physical body. Tension settles in every part of the body, especially in the structural system – the spinal column, as well as the muscles of the shoulders and neck. It also impacts the whole digestive system. In truth, there really is no part of the body that is not strained by this energy. Your spine, nerves, blood, and breath are affected.

What causes this state of resistance that affects your energy so dramatically? Are you purposefully creating this stress in your body? Are you working too hard, doing too much? Is that always what causes stress? Not exactly. It is not how much you do or how hard it is. Resistance is caused by doing things you do not want to do and being with people that you do not want to be with. Your energy goes into a state of resistance when you subconsciously do not want to something, go somewhere, or be with someone.

Resistance is a psychic tension, stubbornly pushing against your actions. You can be either secretive or blatantly loud, conscious, or clueless about your resistance. It does not matter. All are equally bad for your body and state of health. The stronger the state of resistance the more damaging it is to our health.

You could be resisting only your job, but that resistance is so strong it effects every other area of your life. But, just as often, those in a state of resistant energy are resisting their relationship, which, in turn, creates a constant state of resistance in every area of one's life.

Stress comes not from working too long or too hard. Stress is caused by doing too many things that you do not want to do for too long a time. A sense of duty keeps you doing even when you do not want to. Awareness and mindfulness give you the discernment to identify your areas of stress. Discernment tells you which of the stressful areas you could let go or how to change your perception of what you are doing so that you feel joy rather than stress. Faulty perception is responsible for much of our stress. Awareness and discernment allow you to cut through your own delusions and make healthy choices.

You can sense and hear the resistance in others. People display their resistance through their actions and words. The more sensitive can feel the energy of another person's resistance. The more observant can see resistance in another person's body, the stance, the way someone moves is quite telling. Stiff bodies are an indication of stiff thoughts of resistance. People in a state of resistance are more inclined to be judgmental whether to justify their resistance or to ensure that no one around them gets to do what he or she wants either.

Here are a few characteristics of one who is in a state of resistance.

- *You seem angry or frustrated over little things.*
- *You say you will do something, but always back out or are a "no show."*
- *You are quick to judge others.*

- *You do tasks that need to be done, but only after being reminded many times.*
- *You complain a lot.*
- *You overreact with anger at the smallest of things.*
- *Throughout your week, you are more stressed than relaxed.*
- *You procrastinate, big time!*

2. Do I feel as if I want to escape? If so, why?

If you answered "yes," you are in a state of escape or avoidance. While in a state of escape, you are living in a bubble. In this bubble, you are not fully present in your body. In the energy of escape and avoidance, your energy gathers in the mental dimension of thought. Your awareness is not present in the physical body giving rise to the expression "the lights are on, but no one is home."

So, what is one escaping in this energy? This state is a means to avoid the intimacy of physical involvement with people and the world. Instead, you live in the world of thoughts and ideas. Your thought can be anything, positive or negative, about self or others, but it is the thought that is all important and occupies or preoccupies all your time and attention.

Whether a conscious or unconscious choice, those who are escaping, who live in that bubble, have placed a primary importance on thought, the mental dimension of Self. It has nothing to do with the marital status, occupation, or age. When you recognize that someone is "not home" when speaking to them, know that they are in their world of thought. They could be thinking of what they are going to say next instead of listening to you. They could be working out a problem. They could be worrying, creating, or lost in a tornado of confused thought, but they are not present in their body. They are not fully with you. If you are in avoidance, in that bubble, this is what others notice of you.

The energy of escape attracts thoughts and desires of isolation and "alone-ness." The desire to escape creates situations where there is little or no human connection, leaving no opportunity to feel the warmth and fellowship that can pass between people. That bubble of avoidance perpetuates isolation. Over time, the energy of avoidance numbs body sensations, depletes a sense of sensuality, even numbing one to physical pain. People who live in a bubble feel isolated and alone many times because there is no human connection. They isolate in their bubble. They never received the energy of warmth and fellowship that can pass between people because they have shut themselves off from all feeling from others. They have even lost most of their body sensations. They no longer feel their sensuality. Neither do they feel pain because they are cut off from the physical and emotional dimension of their being. They stay in their mental dimension of self.

What is in one's past, in their psyche, in their Inner Child, which brings them to being in a state of avoidance? There are many explanations. Some were raised by parents who lived in a state of avoidance. Children of these parents create their own bubble just to endure the lack of love. For some, the pain of criticism and judgment led to the need to escape. Others just simply prefer living in a bubble, escaping the intimacy of being with others, enjoying their own solitude. Ironically, for some, the feeling of safety while living in a bubble outweighs the feeling of isolation. Some creative thinkers just enjoy their own thoughts.

Whatever the reason, being in the energy of escape has an equally negative effect on the body as does the state of resistance. When in a bubble, your energy is not vitalizing or energizing the physical cells of your body. This withdrawal depletes and eventually diminishes the life force from every organ, gland, muscle – every part of the body, but especially the breath and blood.

Here are some characteristics of being in a state of escape and avoidance.

- *You seem always to be deep in your own thoughts.*
- *Work constantly and think about work continually while at home.*
- *You are always working out a plan in your head.*
- *Other people tell you are a poor listener.*
- *You feel isolated and lonely.*
- *You feel nothing anymore.*
- *You have an addiction or need an intensity, even if painful to feel.*
- *You must always maintain control of yourself, your life.*
- *You do not feel your body temperature, notice the flowers, or see the beauty in our world as you pass by it.*
- *You have numbed your pain to the point where it no longer bothers you even though you still know it is there.*

3. Am I in a state of acceptance?

If you answered "no" to the previous two questions, and your assessment was truthful and sincere, then you are in a state of acceptance, otherwise known as "being in the flow."

When you are in the flow, your heart is expressing its love. Like the sun, you nourish everything and everyone on our planet through the radiation of your energy. There is no need to try, no need to plot, plan, force, or work magic to do this. You simply are a sun. Our Sun does all that it does because of what it is. It is the Sun and that is what a Sun does. It does not resist what it is or escape from what it is. It simply expresses what it is. In the state of acceptance, one has healed old wounds, accepted and forgiven self, others, events, and situations. In so doing, one has removed the negative energy that creates limitation, thus freeing Self to its full and highest potential. Like the Sun, people in the flow can express what is genuine. It is easy to be who they are without excuse or apologies and share their highest being with all they encounter.

People living in a state of acceptance enjoy today and acknowledge the learning of yesterday. They have a positive outlook on tomorrow. People who are "in the flow" naturally create green pastures and golden opportunities. They cannot help but nourish everyone they meet, making others feel good – energized, more positive, lighter. In this energy, the puzzle pieces of life seem to fall into place. There is cooperation at work.

Those "in the flow" are aware, sensitive and know how to concentrate. From this, they can sustain a positive and loving presence. Those "in the flow" are adaptable, flexible, solid, and very much in their physical bodies. They are accepting, not controlling. They accept people as they are, freeing them to be themselves. They are open, honest, and engaged in work that they enjoy, spending time with people. They not only enjoy what they do but carry themselves with confidence and grace while always giving their all. Those "in the flow" feel no threat from the insecurities or power because they feel and know who they are. They allow others to be different from them. They do not blame God for the pain in our world. The Sun gives life to all without reserve, without judgment.

The flow is a fun, creative, ever transforming free state of energy. It is the ultimate reality for those who have chosen the Path! If you are not there yet, know that you can reach this state with determination, concentration, and a willingness to heal.

Let Helen Keller's words inspire you.

> *"Join the company of those who make the barren places of the earth fruitful with kindness. Carry a vision of heaven in your hearts, and you shall make your home, your school, your world corresponds to that vision. Your success and happiness lie within you. External conditions are the accidents of life, its outer trappings. The great*

*enduring realities are love and service. Joy is the holy fire that keeps
our purpose warm and our intelligence aglow.*

*Resolve to keep happy, and your joy and you shall form an invis-
ible host against difficulty. Happiness cannot come from without.
It must come from within. It is not what we see and touch or that
which others do for us which makes up happy; it is that which we
think, feel, and do, first for the other person and then for ourselves."*

Knowledge gives you stamina. Lack of clarity and confusion robs you
of vital energy every day of your life. Knowing your direction and purpose gives you stamina because it carries you towards your vision and
goals.

STEP 7: MEDITATE

*"Most people think there is only darkness behind closed eyes. But
as you develop spiritually and concentrate on the "single" eye in the
forehead, you will find that your inner sight is opened. You will
behold another world, one of many lights and great beauty."*

~Paramanhansa Yogananda, Indian guru

Did you see the word "meditate" and immediately roll your eyes?
Meditation is a powerful tool that anyone can use. Yes, many people struggle with meditation, never believing that they can get quiet
enough to accomplish anything meaningful.

The secret to effective meditation is to not attempt to still your
thoughts, but rather, focus on your awareness of your inner world and
what you sense, see, or feel. We perceive the physical world with our
outer senses, while we perceive our inner world with our inner senses.
Concentrate, pay attention to every subtle thing you sense, feel, see, or

hear. Everything has meaning. If you do not understand, ask why you are seeing this. The answer comes as an intuitive knowing. Continue without questioning or judging the answer. No need to analyze.

Meditation is a joyful time, a time of relaxation, rejuvenation, and spiritual learning. The feelings of unity, harmony, and wisdom that I feel in meditation are now a part of my daily life. Meditation relieves stress. Providing a much-needed sense of well-being and confidence as you walk the Path.

Here are two meditation suggestions.

1. **<u>Being at Peace</u>**

This is a wonderful way to simply be in your positive energy, to feeling your qualities, strength, and purpose. And, since you are already familiar with your Inner Space library, it is easy. Here are the steps in this meditation.

1. While sitting in your favorite chair, or reclining on the bed, close your eyes and feel yourself relaxing.
2. Imaging yourself standing at the front door of your Inner Space library. Go inside. Find the elevator.
3. Once in the elevator, you see a button labelled "Roof."
4. Hit the button to the roof.
5. Feel the elevator rising. You look up over the elevator door and see the arrow indicator moving steadily up, past each floor.
6. As the elevator rises, you feel the energy around you lighten. You are moving into High energy.
7. Then, the elevator stops, the door opens. You step out onto the roof of the library.
8. Look around. This roof contains all the things you need to relax and be.
9. Find a cozy spot and relax. Feel yourself expanding out to connect

with all things in the Universe.

10. Just be in this glorious energy of Love and Oneness.
11. Give yourself time to feel the wonderful energy that is YOU. When you are ready, come back down the elevator and outside the library. Open your eyes.

This is a great meditation to rest and relax, to give your mental side a little break. If you find that thoughts are popping up, create a thought jar on your rooftop. Place your thought in the thought jar until the end of the meditation when you can retrieve them and return.

Also, remember, that going to your Inner Space library, selecting a specific floor, and thumbing through the books and information on that floor to understand yourself is a meditation as well!

2. <u>Higher Travel Meditation</u>

This next method is called Higher Travel because it provides all the benefits of more traditional technique of meditation while also freeing one's awareness to journey into higher dimensions of Self for personal and spiritual growth. I have taught meditation to thousands of individuals. It is a wonderful way to receive guidance, insight, and inspiration, while heightening sensitivity and awareness. It is not imagination but, rather, wisdom from our Inner Space, wisdom that enriches our lives.

Here are the steps for a Higher Travel meditation:

1. Close your eyes and visualize a light about three feet above your head.
2. Feel yourself moving up into this column of light, effortlessly lifting you up higher, freer, and lighter. Consciously feel your awareness lifting in this column of light. Notice what you are sensing and feeling as you rise.
3. Soon you notice that you are sensing a new feeling, a feeling of

expansion, as if you have gone through an opening into a vast expanse.

4. Pay attention to what you are sensing, seeing, and feeling. You will be drawn to certain things that you are sensing or feeling.

5. With each sense or feeling that draws you, ask why you are sensing/feeling this. Ask what message it has for you.

6. Enjoy this high energy. Let the peace surround you.

7. When you are ready, feel yourself floating back down in the column of light until you feel yourself fully back. Open your eyes.

When I do this meditation, I am sensitive to motion and the sense of freedom that I am feeling. I hold my concentration on what I am feeling. As I continue to lift, sometimes I sense color or shades of light. I notice it and continue to feel myself lifting until I begin to feel the energy change. I sense that everything around me is expansive, as if I have gone through an opening into a vast space. Sometimes it feels like harmony far beyond what I feel in my conscious state. Sometimes I sense light in the distance and feel myself moving towards it. Lights, colors, impressions continue to unfold as I focus on whatever is happening.

STEP 8: REACQUAINT YOURSELF WITH NATURE

The greatest profundity is found in simple things. It is so simple to take a walk in the woods and let the birds, crickets and other sounds of nature take precedence over busy thoughts. We all hear the call from time to time.

Henry David Thoreau went to the woods to cultivate and nourish his soul. He responded to the cosmic harmonics that continuously call us to know Self. Every time we go to the woods and listen to the still small voice within us, we have an opportunity to embrace our true self and abilities more fully.

There are numerous ways to "go into the woods." Some are blessed to live close to nature and easily walk in nature. Others find their "woods" on a quiet bench in a nearby park, in a quiet spot in their favorite museum, or in consuming themselves in a creative activity like drawing, in listening to music, or by simply and mindfully washing the dishes.

> *"I went to the woods because I wished to live deliberately, to front only the essential facts of life and see if I could not learn what it had to teach, and not, when I come to die, discover that I had not lived."*
>
> **~Henry David Thoreau**

In the quiet we can seek answers from within – questions asked in silence like:

- Who am I?
- Do I have a purpose for being?
- What is the first thing I should know about myself?
- What is the first thing I must do to strengthen my relationship with my spouse?

Answers will always come quickly as first impressions.

There is a self-empowerment that comes from nature. No more blame. No more resignation. No more isolation. In the woods, you can take responsibility for your life, your happiness, and health. You are free as the wind and can flow towards all good and loving things. When storm clouds appear, there is no need for panic. You can find the source of dark clouds within yourself. You can break up the storm and, once, again, see the sunlight. You can know yourself a little better every day.

STEP 9: KEEP A JOURNAL!

Yes, seriously, keep a journal. Write down what you discover in your evaluations and meditations. There will be days of great self-discovery and there will be days filled with challenges. Document your journey. Know that you are moving toward great awareness of yourself – and, in turn, this will improve your relationship.

STEP 10: WELCOME NEW RELATIONSHIPS AND LET SOME RELATIONSHIPS GO

> *I do my thing, and you do thing, I am not in this world to live up to your expectations, and you are not in this world to live up to mine.*
> *You are you and I am I, and if by chance we find each other, it is beautiful. If not, it cannot be helped.*
> ~**Frederick S. Perl**

As your awareness grows, you will begin to see the truth about your relationships, both your more intimate relationship and relationships with friends and family. Any relationship that does not encourage, support, and nourish is therefore stifling in the limitation and dysfunction it creates. Even relationships that are not necessarily negative but offer little or nothing in the way of vitality can be depleting. True friendship is always a source of healing in one's life. Even intimate relationships are best when they are founded in friendship. Sometimes we maintain negative relationships in our life just because they have always been there, or we are physically dependent on the person through some need. In truth, we are perpetuating a state of isolation.

Negative friends, spouses, bosses, or peers can bring out the worst in us causing us to abuse our power through passive resentment, anger, or even violence. In these situations, we dislike and distrust ourselves.

Nothing takes away our real power faster than self-hatred or the fear of being abusive.

As you walk the Path, you will begin to acknowledge that it is time to let some relationships go. Conversely, you will find that, in your new state of awareness, you will attract new friends, friends with similar awareness and focus. This is inevitable. Welcome these new friends.

Those friends and family members who are still on the Expressway may not understand or like the changes you have made in your life. They may even tell you that you are silly and wasting your time. They have not had the urgings from their own higher Selves as you have, so they do not understand your feelings, perspective, or choices. You will still love them for who they are and where they are on their life journey. True friends and loved ones will love you for who you are, even if they do not fully understand you. Also, you may lovingly part with some friends as your life choices and paths move further apart. You are now in a place where you can embrace new friends when they come into your life or lovingly (and without guilt) let friends go when your life journeys no longer coincide.

When you experience a difference in a relationship but do not know how to put those changes into perspective, the following Relationship Analysis can be helpful. Use this to better understand any relationship – family, friend, neighbor, work colleague. You will want to take notes.

RELATIONSHIP ANALYSIS

1. Identify the friend or family member relationship that you wish to understand.
2. Then answer the following questions. Be honest. Look deeply.
   a. How do I feel when I am with this person?
   b. How does this person bring out my qualities and good nature?

c. How does this person bring out my negative side?
d. Can this relationship be improved?
e. What specific things can I do to stay in my highest energy when I am with this person?

As you read your words from the analysis, you will begin to see how your relationships affect you. You will know which relationships vitalize and empower you and which ones make it difficult to maintain your positive nature.

As you think about your relationships and interactions with others, it is important to remember these key truths:

- It is not your purpose or job to change anyone else.
- You can change how you feel.
- You can have love and compassion for someone, even if it is necessary to discontinue a relationship.
- Every interaction with another person can be based in love and compassion.

Family members can be challenging, depending upon where they are on their life journey. They are dealing with the same issues with Self, the same weakness, hurts, and habits. They are where they are. Here are some examples of a challenging relationship with parents and in-laws.

- *You have nothing in common with your parents except your chromosomes.*
- *You have nothing in common with your in-laws except for your spouse.*
- *Attempts at pleasant conversations are stiff and awkward.*
- *They frequently tell you what is wrong with you.*
- *They frequently criticize how you do things and tell you how you **should** do things.*
- *They frequently criticize others you love – particularly your spouse or children.*

- *They are simply unhappy with you, others, and life.*
- *It is uncomfortable to be around their unhappiness.*

Negative parents and in-laws can be draining on vitality, always leaving you feeling tired, to the point where you dread spending time with them. There could be many other reasons your relationship is strained, but the bottom line is that it is not pleasant to visit. Completely removing them from your life is nearly impossible, so what do you do?

Remember, you cannot change them. It is impossible. You may have even tried before and failed. While you cannot change them, nor should you try, you can change how you feel and react when you are with them. The secret is in the preparation. These preparation steps work.

HEART COOKIES

In preparation, consider using something called a Heart Cookie. You can silently send a Heart Cookie to someone at any time. It is easy. Consciously feel the love in your heart, imagine that love forming into a round shape like a cookie, then send that Heart Cookie to someone. Imagine your love surrounding that person. Know that your Heart Cookie is nourishing its recipient with love and compassion. That recipient may be in the room or thousands of miles away. Heart Cookies make it easier for you even if you are in the middle of an encounter with someone. Heart Cookies can also be sent ahead of time, in anticipation of an interaction. You will be surprised how effective your Heart Cookies are.

Heart Cookies take you to your Loving Self energy. When you are in your heart, your love is flowing, you interact with others through your Loving Self. In this higher energy, nothing negative can impact your energy system. All energy is flowing outward.

From that Loving Self, you can use these helpful techniques.

- Send each family member a Heart Cookie, whether they are difficult or not. It will change the mood of the interactions.
- When your family member criticizes you, do not shrink or argue. Simply respond with humor. For example, your in-law says, "God, you look awful!" You can respond, "What can I do? I was born this way!" And let out a laugh.
- Change the subject by saying something positive you noticed about him/her.
- Let go of the need to disagree, defend, or be right. No need to play their game. Responding from a place of love always deflates the negative.
- Imagine that you can see their Inner Child who is wounded and needs love. Their criticism and negative remarks are most likely coming from a wounded Inner Child. Knowing this, you can easily let go of the desire to blurt out a negative response.
- Remember, that you know you! You are not the things that are being criticized or judged, therefore, you do not have to accept them. You can detach from them with love.

Work relationships are obviously influenced by the work environment. In a negative work environment, egos jostle for attention, critics knit-pick, devious co-workers might even sabotage the work of others. Interactions of this type of environment are often filled with judgment, dirty looks, passive aggressive responses, and other behavior that perpetuate disharmony and distrust. Sadly, some will carry this negative energy and behavior home, only to take their frustration out on their loved ones. How draining – to the Sexual Self, to the other Selves!

Heart Cookies work in the business environment, just as they work for personal situations. When you get to work and are settled, silently feel your heart and Loving Self. Imagine a huge Heart Cookie forming, then send waves of warmth, love, and compassion throughout your entire work area. Feel the waves lifting all negativity up through the ceiling. Feel your warmth and loving feeling moving towards others in the work area who have been contributing to the negative work environment. Think of something good about each person. You can do this quietly with your eyes open. It takes only a few minutes.

Send a Heart Cookie to the work area throughout the day. Do this every day. On the third day, notice the differences in the environment. Send Heart Cookies as needed. Do this without telling anyone. It benefits everyone in the work area. Knowing that your love and compassion makes a silent difference is reward enough.

Most of all, in every situation, feel good about yourself. Whether your family members, friends, or work colleagues are consciously aware of it, you will have added some sunshine to their lives. You have the means to create loving situations in all aspects of your life. Love is a primal force of life. Choose to be and attract love and compassion.

$$\approx\approx$$

Above all, remember, YOU GOT THIS! You can do this. You can restore balance within yourself which brings about balance in your life. A healthy Sexual Self and the relationships that unfold with a healthy Sexual Self are possible. Intimacy that ensures sex on Saturday night is possible. You got this!

Be kind to yourself as you take this journey. You made the very brave choice to live your life in a new way. That desire and intention is the foundation of your success. You made the choice for joy and peace of mind. You made the choice for a loving relationship with your partner. And, as you know, we manifest in our life our thoughts, feelings, desires, and intentions.

For every drop of rain there are millions of rays of sunshine. Both are vital to the existence of life on our planet. Both are vital to each of us. If the proportion of raindrops to sunshine were reversed or even varied to a small degree, all life would be threatened. The balance of nature is exacting in its preservation of life.

Like nature, we too must be exacting in maintaining balance. Drops of rain cleanse. purify and keep us adaptable and pliable. They are the test and challenges that sometime blur our vision and cloud our insight. They are the learning experiences that help us to mature and spiritually evolve. Rays of sunshine nourish our physical, emotional, mental, and spiritual bodies with light and life-giving qualities. They are the good times – the loving, peaceful, and joyful times. These moments are meant to be a million times more frequent than the drops of rain for the balance to be life-sustaining. Our physical health, as well as our emotional, mental, and spiritual health, is dependent on an exact balance of drops of rain and rays of sunshine.

A friend and student at Delphi University, Holly Yeda, shared this poem. It sums up the message in this chapter.

You are wiser than you know
more courageous than you guess.
You are stronger than you feel.
In the greatness of your soul.
You are younger than your years.
You are beautiful to see.
You can hold your joy
underneath the complete emotions of tears.
You have loved beyond your dreams
far more special than you think.
You are one with the Divine.
Life is kinder than it seems.

Child of God, accept that love with
singing through your mind.
Every miracle is yours.
You are wonderful.
Believe.

We all can create our life as we envision it. We have an incredible strength of spirit, an intense will, and a multitude of abilities available to use. Negative weight blocks our perception of these resources. As the negative weight begins to peel off, much like peeling an onion skin, the radiance of our light begins to shine. The love that we are begins to express itself. One cannot be healed within self without becoming a facilitator of healing. Love desires to share all that is good. Abundance becomes a way of life. As we begin to know the many aspects of Self, we can address each of them, one by one, and begin the healing process. When we begin removing the negative weight, our awareness shifts to the probability and possibility of making positive life changes. The path leads us to new horizons and the realization that no matter how small we think we are in this vast universe; we can make a difference.

Chapter Five:

———— ✺ ————

MAINTAINING THE THRILL, LIFE WITH A HEALTHY SEXUAL SELF

WELL, BY NOW you are realizing that the investment you have made in healing your Selves was well worth it, and you are reaping the benefits of a creative life with your partner, a life without the unnecessary and stressful drama. You are empowered! You live an empowered life.

You have all you need to create and nurture a deeply loving relationship. You have all you need to take sex on Saturday night to new heights on a physical, emotional, and spiritual level. You now have an opportunity to maintain that thrill that only comes from a deep connection with your partner.

In this chapter, we discuss several tangible things that you can do to maintain the thrill. But keep in mind that by making the choice to walk the Path and to heal your Sexual Self, your relationship with your partner cannot help but grow and expand in wonderful, deeply loving ways. By healing all your energy center Selves, you now live from your Heart. You see people and things differently. You behave differently. Your essence of compassion and love can only attract positive things.

THE LASTING RELATIONSHIP

Have you ever encountered a couple who were obviously in love, who expressed that love in both verbal and non-verbal ways, who seemed to interact together with such harmony that the flow was obvious even to the casual observer? There is an energetic connection with such couples that is tangible. They have an authentic bonding, not an ego-based bonding.

Caring and loving relationships have several things is common. But they always start with love – true, heart-felt love. A deep, true, heart-felt love extends to all aspects of a relationship – physical, emotional, and spiritual. These couples have a relationship that exists and thrives on all levels:

- Physical: Body language confirms the closeness of a couple. They lean toward each other, often lightly touching, eyes connecting. There is no doubt of their love, no doubts that inhibit fulfilling sex on Saturday night.
- Mental: There is an unspoken understanding among couples who are deeply in love. They "get" each other. They can easily talk, share, debate, challenge, knowing they will be understood.
- Emotional: Each partner shows his/her feelings not only in their words, but also in their actions. Partners feel connected and wanted. Each partner feels seen, feels understood, and feels wanted.
- Spiritual: Couples have chemistry. There is a connection greater and deeper than all others.

Love is an interesting word, a word that can be misused or misunderstood. I have heard it said that people are driven by one of two basic motivations – achievement or purpose – or, in other words, the ego or the heart. There are many reasons that we might partner out of emotional need or ego, reasons that we confuse for love. For example:

- The man who marries the "trophy wife" and feels his self-esteem grow when other men ogle her.
- The woman who has a "sugar daddy" who showers her with luxurious gifts that are the envy of her friends.
- The single parent who marries because the children need a mother or father.
- The single person who is lonely and commits to a partner to find companionship.
- The person who does not love their partner but shrugs their shoulders and thinks "at least I have a roof over my head, and food on the table."

Why do people choose to come together in a relationship? What brings two people together? The first response is "love, of course." But is it that love "purposeful, from-the-heart" love? Or is it that "you fill a gap in my self-worth" love? Does that love come from a bruised Self (Ego) or does it come from the heart? By now, having read the previous chapters and having taken your personal steps to be in a healthy and loving place, you are beginning to understand and see the difference.

True, heart-felt love is based upon purpose, rather than achievement or status. That is, its purpose is the mutual caring and giving that nourishes both partners, providing a means for both partners to grow in their love and awareness of the joys of life. Neither partner is there to fix, change, parent, or scold the other. They are together because of their mutual love and desire to be together.

Partners in a caring and loving relationship not only hear the words, "I love you," but feel the words "I love you." Feeling is believing. Each partner must believe in his/her love for the other – and believe and trust that this love is mutual.

Expressing feelings is a natural part of a caring and loving relationship. It is easy to express love for each other in verbal and non-verbal ways – after all, actions speak louder than words. It is easy and safe to share unpleasant feelings because caring and loving partners know and trust their deep love. Not every moment of every day will be ideal. But partners in a caring and loving relationship know, beyond any doubt, that they will work things out, that, together, they will face and overcome every challenge.

Partners genuinely enjoy being with each other. Spouses take precedent over the frequent happy hour with co-workers. Social media and television take a back seat to conversation and personal interaction. There is genuine enjoyment in being together and doing things together. Caring and loving partners are considerate and thoughtful. Doing for your partner comes naturally, feels effortless. It is easy to share chores and family responsibilities. In a caring and loving partnership, one knows when their partner is overextended or tired, stepping in to help without being asked.

You are well on the way to this type of relationship. It is more than possible, especially now that you have a healthy Sexual Self and healthy energy center Selves. So, what tangible things you can do to maintain and enhance your relationship. Here are a few suggestions.

MISTAKES HAPPEN, FORGIVE!

By empowering your life as you have done, you are undoubtedly realizing that you can forgive your past mistakes and transgressions because you now understand the true You and all your Selves.

You know that you would never willingly hurt yourself or others. Does that mean we never make any more mistakes? No. While you may make fewer mistakes, mistakes are inevitable. With a healthy Sexual Self and other Selves, you no longer act from a place of self-centered thoughtlessness, insensitivity, aggression, impatience, and other negative places. You can now make a conscious decision to repair the mistake and heal the hurt. You are now in a place where you can forgive yourself and others. Forgiveness is an important foundation of an empowered life.

Make Choices from a Loving Heart

Your personal empowerment encompasses much more than simply your day-to-day activities. You have awakened the vital life force within your body and all its energy centers. Why is this important? You now perceive the world from a higher perspective. You see above the drama and ego. *You see the Big Picture.*

From this expanded view of your life, the world, and events in your world, you are now equipped to make healthy and wise decisions, decisions for the greatest good of all involved. You can more easily know where you are and what direction you should take. You can easily see the mountains and, if your goal is on the other side of the mountain, you will know to prepare for the journey and pack for the climb. More importantly, with this clarity and new perspective, you understand that molehills are truly just molehills, not giant insurmountable mountains that hinder your progress at every turn. Seeing molehills in their true proportion allows you to handle daily activities and face each encounter with ease and simplicity.

Physical vitality, greater clarity, stronger sense of purpose, less drama, feeling that life has meaning – all this sounds wonderful! Who would not want to have clarity of perception, the ability to face each day with purpose in life, and a peace that comes from rising about the drama and turmoil? Yet, most people are living only a very small portion of their potential. Most people are mired in the dense, distracting energies brought about by negative thoughts and feelings.

You have chosen not to be "most people." You have chosen to awaken your potential. From this place, your relationship cannot help but grow in its vitality and intimacy. Sex on Saturday night, when surrounded in high energy, not only enhances the physical activity of sex, but strengthens the spiritual bond with your partner.

> *A person who does not know but knows that he does not know is a student; teach him.*
>
> *A person who knows but who does not know that he knows is asleep; awaken him.*
>
> *But a person who knows and knows that he knows is wise; follow him.*
>
> **Old Asian Proverb**

From a place of empowerment, you will clearly see life's path and your destination. There is no going back! You will know the moment you have stepped off the Path, as well as the moment you need to step back on the Path. You will immediately recognize when a less-aware person in your life tries to persuade you off your Path. You will become acutely aware that you have a choice. You are free to assess your direction at any moment and make a new choice.

Succumbing to lower energy is a conscious choice. Choices are much easier to make in the clear light of wisdom, from that higher perspective. Poor choices are the unfortunate result of the unclear, less precise, blurry insight of an unempowered, unaware individual. With the higher insight of empowerment and enlightenment, you will generally seek the fellowship of others who are traveling the same Path. While you still care about your old friends and colleagues, you will now recognize that you are no longer hindered or seduced by their words and desires. You can fully understand that old friends are free to choose their path just as we are free to choose ours. This is a powerful and freeing realization.

As our higher energy centers awaken, our vitality awakens, bringing with it new possibilities and directions never envisioned. Remember the vulture story. Sending the black clouds away and letting the light surround and envelop your thoughts empowers your soul. Our Spirit becomes free to fill our life with compassion, humility, integrity, and creative genius.

Taking one aware step at a time keeps you from running over others who are also learning. The compassion taught by your own wounds allows you to stop and talk to the heart of another. Commitment to the Path of self-enlightenment frees you to discover your purpose and express the gifts of your soul.

KNOW YOUR PRIORITIES.

Take a minute to review how your actions reflect your priorities. Naturally, actions that secure our safety and survival have a high priority – we work, earn an income, have a place to live, and buy groceries. You would do these things if you were single or in a relationship. But, beyond these basic priorities, what do your actions say about the priority you give your relationship?

Certain behaviors are blaring indications that the relationship is less than top priority, such as:

- Spending more time with friends and co-workers than with your partner, such as, frequent nights out with the "guys."
- Giving more attention to social media or television than to your partner.
- Wanting only mental sex, that is, sex with no intimacy, just "wham-bam-thank you-ma'am" and roll over to sleep.
- Offering no help with chore or the children.
- Frequently cheating in a non-physical way, as in, obviously ogling or fantasizing about someone.

In caring and loving relationships, one's partner and family effortlessly come first. Look, no one is perfect. However, frequent behavior that avoids interaction or is insensitive to your partner are clear red flags. What does your behavior say about your priorities?

CHECK IN ON OUR SELVES WHEN NEEDED.

There will be times when you feel out of sorts without an understanding of the cause. In times like these, it is easy to find yourself being pulled into family or work drama and responding in reactive (and often negative) ways. Of course, whatever the source and reasons, feeling out of sorts has an impact on one's relationship.

In cases like this, it helps to identify which of your seven major Selves may be causing trouble. What are you experiencing?

- The Presence – Do you see a phony smile when you look in the mirror?
- The Emotional Self / Inner Child – Are you becoming easily drawn into drama? Are you creating the drama?
- The Achiever Self – Are you feeling a strong need to control the situation? Are you feeling others are beneath you?

- The Loving Self – Are you feeling unusually disappointed in things?
- The Creative Expressor – Are you unusually quiet, or saying things you would not usually say?
- The Intuitive Self / Visionary – Are you judging yourself?
- The Angel – Do you feel disconnected from your Higher Source (by whatever name you call that Higher Source)?

Once identified, re-evaluate, and restore that troublesome Self to a healthy state, using the guided visualization described in Chapter 4.

READ THE SIGNS.

Be aware of the emotional and energetic state of your partner. As you walk the Path, this will become easier to do, eventually requiring no effort. Is your partner behaving out of sorts? Is their behavior indicating that they want or need something that is not being expressed? With practice you can identify whether your partner is in masculine or feminine energy, or in archetypal energy, or exhibiting a troublesome Self. Knowing this information will guide how, when, and if you approach your partner. Sometimes your partner simply needs some space or maybe even a hug. Sometimes the situation requires that you be a caring and loving listener. Knowing your partner's signs helps you to interact in a caring and loving way.

This same situation also applies to your extended sphere of influences – your children, family, neighbors, and work colleagues.

INTIMACY IS MORE THAN PHYSICAL.

We understand that lovemaking is an act of intimacy. Interestingly, intimacy is also defined as closeness, togetherness, affinity, rapport, warmth, and affection. Intimacy is more than physical. It is sometimes best expressed in the little things like giving your partner your undivided attention. When your smartphone is secondary to your conversation, you can make and maintain eye contact. Not only is that an intimate interaction, but it is also a powerful non-verbal way to show your love.

There are many ways to be intimate that do not involve sex. Impromptu foot rubs, doing house chores without being asked, cooking a favorite dish are just a few examples. Of course, whispering "I love you" at an unexpected moment, when spoken in earnest, evokes a deeply intimate feeling.

Of course, non-physical intimacy, when express sincerely and with feeling, always makes for better sex on Saturday night.

COMMUNICATE WITH LOVE

Communicate from a place of love rather than a place of anger and accusation. Good therapists often encourage couples to use "I feel" statements, not only during therapy sessions but also in daily life. This form of communication eliminates any accusatory or judgmental tones in the communication, enabling heart-felt discussion. When discussing an issue, start by describing how you feel when the issue/action occurs. For example, rather than saying, "You care more about going out with the guys than you do about me," use an "I feel" statement like "I feel alone and forgotten when you go out with the guys."

Using "I feel" statements also provide an opportunity to state what you want or need. While what you want to happen may not be the ultimate outcome, it does provide an opportunity for discussion and resolution. For example, using the example from above, "I feel alone and forgotten when you go out with the guys. I would like to be invited to go, too."

As you communicate, send a Heart Cookie. Know that you speak from your heart, that you desire a resolution for the highest and greatest good for both you and your partner.

BREAK OLD UNHEALTHY HABITS

As you live a loving and healthy life, you may realize that it is time to change some old habits that contribute little to your life or relationships. It may be time to remove some of these habits, especially those that no longer bring a sense of satisfaction and purpose. By letting go of the old, you have the capacity to embrace the new. These are behaviors that, when overextended, become more of an escape mechanism than a fun, enjoyable activity.

Hobbies and Projects

Do a quick assessment. How much enjoyment do you get from your hobbies and projects? Do you maintain a hobby or project that is more draining than it is vitalizing? Are there any hobbies and projects that you continue because you feel you "should" or "must?"

If you are no longer excited about that project, then it is time to let it go, pass the torch to someone else. By letting it go, you free yourself to attract a new creative endeavor, a new opportunity to learn, grow, and feel a sense of satisfaction, a new opportunity to include those close to you. When is the right time to let go? There are no rules – what is right for you is right for you! There is only one guideline – any project, hobby, or extra activity that no longer provides a sense of fulfillment and joy in your life, let it go. Lovingly release yourself knowing this will free you for your next opportunity, whatever it may be.

Doing for Others

Do you find yourself wrapped up is other people's stuff? This, too, is a habit based upon emotional need. The "prior you" may have sought approval and feelings of worth by staying busy doing for others. Yes, of course, doing for others is a good thing unless doing for others is motivated by a desire to be accepted or loved – or, from a sense of superiority and control. When doing for others has reached the point where you feel like an unappreciated, high-class slave, then it is time to make a change. It is time to learn how to say "no."

Remember that saying "no" is sometimes the most loving thing you can do – not only for yourself but for others. It is healthy to set boundaries. When you say "no" to someone, you put the accountability, responsibility, and consequences of choice back in the appropriate hands. Ironically, while it may be painful to say "no," it is a very healthy thing to do. Family of addicts understand how important saying "no" can be to recovery– it is called tough love.

Make a list of all the things you do for people that they could do themselves. After all, how are they going to learn the satisfaction and self-esteem that comes from taking responsibility for their needs? Where appropriate, lovingly tell those on your list that you will be taking time for yourself and can no longer do what you have been doing for them. There is no need for anger, criticism, or judgment. Use the additional time to not only nurture yourself, but to also nurture your relationship.

Daily Routines of Life

Regulated, unadulterated "creature habit" routine is an addiction that enslaves your freedom and limits opportunity for creative adventure. Whether the routine is coming home from work, having two cocktails before dinner, playing that new video game, streaming your usual shows, and falling asleep — or going out to the local sports bar every night. Any hardcore, consistent routine depletes your creative juices. Routines do not require thought. You can be a mental zombie – heck, you have mastered this routine, it is so effortless, you do not even have to think. No thinking, no creativity, no enthusiasm, nor motivation is required when a routine is a substitute for life.

Some routines are necessary. We must maintain our hygiene, take care of our health, feed the dog. The typical daily life is filled with routines that we no longer even give focused thought. Take our morning routine as an example. Getting up in the morning, combing your hair and looking in the mirror, shaving or putting on makeup. Often, we do these things without really seeing ourselves or how we really look. Pay attention. Be consciously aware of yourself and your actions. If you are aware that you feel good about yourself and how you look, you will automatically benefit others and your world. Your energy will flow. You will be more accepting of others because you feel good about yourself. When you look in that mirror, look into your eyes. See the beauty of your Spirit, see the spark of your creativity, your humor. Know that about you every morning. Let yourself shine.

Spontaneity is the inspiration of genius in many aspects of life, including the bedroom. Change things up. Brush your teeth before you brush your hair. Dance to the closet. Flirt with yourself. Play with a strand of hair. Feel your gentle beauty. When you get dressed for the day, consciously choose clothing that you feel matches today's energy and focus. Go out into the world and share your spirit and good feelings.

Breaking routine to try something new and different, even if it is as simple as reading a good book, can stimulate new direction and add zip to your energy system. Awareness of Self means empowering all the Selves.

The Perfect Home, the Perfect Everything

Do you spend all your free time cleaning your house, or making every drawer and closet meticulously organized? Do you worry than your shirt looks a little wrinkled or your daughter's pigtails were uneven? Perfectionists suffer the disease of lack. Nothing is ever quite good enough. Everything must be perfect. As you continue your journey of healing and self-discovery, you realize that your home does not have to be perfect, but it does have to feel warm, inviting, in harmony. Spending time on your self-discovery is much more valuable than an organized sock drawer or hunting down every speck of dirt!

When you are focused on the dust bunny in the corner, or the knick-knacks that are not evenly spaced on the shelf, you miss the Big Picture. You overlook the sunlight streaming through the window, the pleasant aroma of the honeysuckle vine outside the window, the delicious smell of your spouse as they walk by you. Neither will you recognize any other creative opportunities to nourish your soul. Your sense of Self, your self-esteem and self-worth, comes from within, not on how clean your house is or how manicured your lawn is.

I knew a woman who consciously placed her activities with family before her housecleaning. If someone pointed out a cobweb or a dusty shelf in her home, she would quickly say, "Don't touch it. It's a science experiment." Then, she would laugh and enjoy life. Let go of the idea of a spotless, organized home. Allow yourself to see the Big Picture. Cleaning has its place, but do not forget to be mindful of the beauty of each moment throughout your day.

Imagine what your relationship would be like if you let the perfectionism go and focused on your spouse, really saw your spouse from a warm place in your heart!

Work, Work, Work

Even when you have healed the Achiever of its laser-beam focus on work and achieving, it is equally challenged to give up the habit of work. If it has been the focus of your attention and energy, it can be just as challenging when it is time to change your usual, habitual, work routine. The first step to letting go of this habit is to limit work to the workplace, whatever that workplace may be. Then, leave the mental focus at your workplace when the workday is over. If you work in the home, allow yourself ample time to do your work (whether it is housekeeping or remote work), then consciously tell yourself when you workday is over. Now is it time to play, to do something you enjoy doing, enjoying your family and friends. That Inner Child of yours must have time to play. Vitality is released within every dimension of your being when you are doing something you love. No duty or responsibility is involved. The sheer enjoyment of doing something you love empowers you and fuels your spirit.

Think about what you could do in the home or outside that would be enjoyable. Get to know your quirky nuances, to value your sense of humor, to feel your big, beautiful heart. Free your thoughts and make a list of not only the things you enjoy but the things you would like to try, things you might enjoy. Then, start small, do one thing on your list. You get to know yourself even better by trying new things to see if you really enjoy them. If you try something and discover that it is just not for you, then now you know. Move on the next one. We learn from the experiences.

FIND "TOGETHER" ACTIVITIES.

Finding "together" activities is easier than you may think. Start with household responsibilities. At a minimum, you can share the household chores, but, where possible, find a time during the week where you can do your chores together. You will be surprised how this can strengthen your relationship.

Discover activities that you both enjoy and make a point to do them regularly. What activity do both you and your partner enjoy, an activity that can be done together? There are activities at home (other than chores) than you can share such as gardening, playing cards or board games, having an "at home" date night. And, of course, there are a wealth of activities outside the home that you can enjoy together such as outdoor concerts, bike riding, hiking, picnics, museums, historical sights – the list goes on and on.

Discover your common interests. Or, explore new interests together. Make a conscious effort to do "together" activities at least once a month!

$$\sim\!\!\sim$$

At one time, there was a popular meme that said, "Transcend Yourself. Transcend the World." While this is a powerful message, I feel something is missing. I believe it should read, "Transcend Yourself. Heal your relationships. Transcend the World."

Thanks for letting me share the findings of my lifelong studies. You now have the information and tools to be the fullness of who you are, to express your creativity, to be inspired and to inspire others, and to fully, deeply love and be loved. You are the master of your life. You have the means to create a beautiful, rewarding life. I can feel the smile on your face and your excitement as you anticipate Sex on Saturday Night.

Go for it!

Patrcia Hayes Smith

ACKNOWLEDGEMENTS

Several years ago, with my husband's encouragement, I drafted a manuscript about relationships. He jokingly called it "Sex on Saturday Night," and the name stuck. It was "put on the back burner" as life events, our school, Delphi University, and other activities took priority.

When it was time to dust off the manuscript and move forward with its completion and publication, there were several individuals who helped make that happen.

- Of course, I want to thank my husband, Marshall Smith, for his loving encouragement. He was a patient listener and always offered sound advice as I was writing. Thanks, Babe, for continuing to inspire me, even from the Afterlife.
- Thank you, Melissa Ann Creel, for your thorough proofreading and meaningful comments. Despite a heavy work schedule and knowing little about the book beforehand, you dove right in. You have a gift for detail...and grammar.
- I also want to thank my granddaughter, Charee Schubert, for making time in her busy schedule to read the manuscript with the eye of the contemporary young adult. Your feedback was most helpful.
- My daughter, Kelly, has been such a steady and reliable help to

me. You are an amazing daughter even when we try each other's patience. In your way, you have helped to keep this project moving. I am deeply grateful for you and for the many things you do for me. I love you.

- It is important to mention the hundreds of clients who sought my help over the years, who chose to heal themselves and their relationships. In so doing, they have contributed to my understanding of our psyche and ways to heal. My clients have proven how effective the guidance in this book really is. Thank you!

- Lastly, I want to thank Elizabeth Hood. She hung out with me and made me laugh. Seriously, she helped me organize and finalize the contents of this book. And we had a great time doing it. I will be forever grateful for her love and friendship.

About the Author

Patricia Hayes Smith is a renowned spiritual educator, therapist, author, and speaker. A graduate of Nova University with a degree in Behavioral Science, Patricia has devoted her career to developing and teaching alternative therapies and healing modalities. Along with her husband, Marshall Smith, Patricia founded Delphi University of Spiritual Studies. She is known for her innovative class subjects, therapies, and experiential teaching style. Patricia has taught thousands of students in alternative healing modalities and ancient philosophies. She has been a guest lecturer and conducted workshops for corporations, medical associations, and organizations for business professionals.

Truly a pioneer in alternative studies and related subjects, Patricia has authored seven books on related topics. During her long career, she has participated in several research projects including research conducted by Dr. William Roll with the Parapsychology Laboratory at Duke University, research with dolphins conducted by the University of Miami, and, along with Marshall Hayes, assisted archeologists from the University of South Carolina. Patricia is credited with providing key research that led to the identification of right brain development as the source of intuitive intelligence.

Patricia presently resides in the mountains of North Georgia where she continues to write and develop innovative methods of bringing enlightened awareness to all.

Other Books by
Patricia Hayes Smith

The Definitive Book on the Afterlife, Outskirts Press, Inc, 2020

This extraordinary book documents the events of her husband's passing. Through meditation, Marshall Smith, detailed what happened the moment he passed, where he went, and what he is doing now. In addition, the book outlines how to communicate with your loved ones who have passed and how to prepare your place in the Afterlife. It offers reassurance and peace, eliminating the fear of dying.

What is RoHun? The Wisdom of Self-Discovery, Dog Ear Publishing, 2017

In the mid 1980's Patricia Hayes developed a powerful transpersonal psychotherapy process called RoHun™. This book describes RoHun™, its healing processes, and its positive healing effects. A must-read for those who are looking to make real and lasting changes in their lives.

Lights From the Heavens / I'll Never Stop Loving You, self-published, 2014

This book is two books in one, intertwined among Patricia's beautiful Entura artwork. It shares an unusual and deeply profound love story that will challenge your belief system while it tugs at your heart strings. Lights from the Heavens confirms the truth and power of true love and gives hope and inspiration to those have lost faith that true love exists. A visual and heart-felt wonder!

Prince Abba and Magi Patiput: The Adventures of Prince Abba, Dog Ear Publishing, 2010

In this magical and mystical tale, we follow the adventures of the orphaned and imprisoned intuitive, Prince Abba, and his Master Teacher, Magi Patiput, as Abba discovers the realities of the world and, in the process, discovers his intuitive talents and abilities. The Storyteller weaves an exciting tale of challenges and meaningful encounters of love and life along Prince Abba's journey to knowing himself. A magical way for adults to learn important spiritual truths.

Extension of Life: Channelings by Arthur Ford, co-authored by Marshall Smith, Dimensional Brotherhood Publishing House, 1986

In this book, Patricia and Marshall share the wisdom of Arthur Ford, famous medium and spiritual teacher. It expands your thinking beyond traditional views of life and death, demonstrating that consciousness survives physical death. You will never look at life and death the same way.

The Gatekeeper, co-authored by Marshall Smith, Dimensional Press, 1981

This book documents a series of messages that Patricia Hayes received from several beings including the Gatekeeper, who not only shares his deep and insightful knowledge but who also coordinates Patricia's communication with other beings with messages to share. Topics range from health, diet, and sex to the workings of the Universe. The Gatekeeper will inspire you with his powerful, magical, and practical messages.

ABOUT DELPHI UNIVERSITY, SCHOOL OF SPIRITUAL STUDIES

Co-founded by Patricia Hayes and Marshall Smith, Delphi University has been offering metaphysical healing and transpersonal psychotherapy training since the mid-1980s, and more recently, has expanded its curriculum to include intuitive art therapy training.

Located in the Blue Ridge Mountains near the Cherokee National Forest, Delphi's beautiful, natural surroundings is a perfect environment for spiritual studies. Students can hear the river and the rustle of the trees as they study. Campus facilities include classroom buildings and student housing nestled among the trees. The Church of Wisdom and Mauricio Panisset Healing Sanctuary are open to students and the surrounding community.

In additional to the therapies and modalities that students take with them, Delphi University is a wonderful and peaceful place to get to know one's self, to explore new truths, and to reach new heights in spiritual awareness.

For more information, visit our website, at www.delphiu.com.

CPSIA information can be obtained
at www.ICGtesting.com
Printed in the USA
LVHW031917171222
735440LV00029B/512